Heart-warming
HYMN STORIES

Heart-warming
HYMN STORIES

by Dr. Lindsay Terry

Post Office Box 1099 • Murfreesboro, Tennessee 37133

Printed and Bound in the United States of America

To Gladys Wilbar, my mother-in-law, who, at ninety-three years of age, continues to be a great encouragement to me. Through the years she was a source of strength for her husband, Russell Wilbar, now deceased, and continues to uphold, love and regard her children, Aleck and Marilyn.

Story Contents

Story Contents

Story Contents

Story Contents

Story Contents

Song Contents

Song Contents

Song Contents

Preface

For many years I have delighted in the study of the stories behind our famous hymns and gospel songs. I have found that many, if not most, were born out of human suffering. Out of a dark period in the life of one of God's children, suddenly there springs forth a ray of light, a sunbeam—a song!

I have gleaned these stories from conversations with those wonderful songwriters, from friends who knew them and from periodicals and books of hymnology.

Although this book is primarily a devotional volume, the contents can be used as sermon illustrations, Sunday school lesson illustrations or story backgrounds for youth or children's gatherings. Schoolteachers have often found them to be exciting to their students.

Other volumes of this nature that I have written have proven to be spiritual helps, and I trust that these additional stories will bring further blessings to the readers. May these stories cause greater glory to come to the Lord Jesus Christ each time you hear one of these wonderful hymns.

Adoring Christ

All Hail the Pow'r of Jesus' Name

Philippians 2:1–11

"Wherefore God also hath highly exalted him, and given him a name which is above every name."—Vs. 9.

I would rank this as the greatest hymn of praise in the English language:

> **All hail the pow'r of Jesus' name!**
> **Let angels prostrate fall.**
> **Bring forth the royal diadem**
> **And crown Him Lord of all.**

Edward Perronet, the writer of this hymn, was a close associate of John and Charles Wesley. He was born in England in 1726 and was educated for the ministry in the Church of England, following his father and grandfather in this profession.

He objected to many of the practices of the church, leaning strongly to the doctrines of the Wesleys. He even advocated the starting of a new denomination, but the Wesleys would not break their ties with the Anglican Church.

Mr. Perronet was a strong, impulsive, self-willed individual; therefore, he pulled out and started an independent church in Canterbury. Shortly after Edward Perronet established his church, he wrote this famous hymn, which was published in 1780 in the *Gospel Magazine,* edited by Augustus Toplady. A few years later those same verses appeared in a book of poems by an anonymous author. One of the poems was written as an acrostic, the letters of which spelled *Edward Perronet*. Most of his work was done under an assumed name or no name at all.

The tune "Coronation," which is just as popular as the verses, was written by one of America's most noted hymn tune writers, Oliver Holden. He composed it during a time of great rejoicing—when his wife presented him with a fine baby girl. The four-and-a-half-octave organ on which he composed the tune is still displayed in the Old State House in Boston.

In church services today, you may hear these verses sung to three tunes: "Coronation," "Miles Lane" or "Diadem." "Coronation" is by far the most popular.

England and America came together in the persons of Edward Perronet and Oliver Holden and gave to the world the hymn, "All Hail the Power of Jesus' Name." The third stanza reads:

> **Let ev'ry kindred, ev'ry tribe,**
> **On this terrestrial ball,**
> **To Him all majesty ascribe**
> **And crown Him Lord of all.**

Reflection: Christ left His majestic position and condescended to provide salvation for lowly human beings. May He enjoy an exalted position in our hearts today. He and only He is worthy to be Lord of all.

Alone in the Big City

My Faith Looks Up to Thee

Hebrews 11:1–16

"Now faith is the substance of things hoped for, the evidence of things not seen."—Vs. 1.

Many of our hymns were composed as Christians wrote exactly what they felt in their hearts at the time. Such was the case in the writing of "My Faith Looks Up to Thee."

Ray Palmer, fresh out of Yale, went to New York to teach school for a while. One very discouraging year he battled illness and loneliness. One night he sat down in his room to put in verse form the feelings of his heart, which he had done since childhood. This night the Lord seemed particularly near and dear to him, and he began to write:

> **My faith looks up to Thee,**
> **Thou Lamb of Calvary,**
> **Saviour divine!**
> **Now hear me while I pray;**
> **Take all my guilt away;**
> **Oh, let me from this day**
> **Be wholly Thine!**

On and on he wrote until four stanzas were completed. He copied them from the single sheet into his pocket notebook so he could refer to them when he needed a lift, never intending for anyone else to see them.

Several months later Ray Palmer met Dr. Lowell Mason on a street in Boston. Dr. Mason asked him to furnish some hymns for a hymnal that he and Dr. Hastings were about to publish. For the first time, Mr. Palmer displayed his poem. Dr. Mason stepped into a store and hurriedly copied the words on another sheet of paper. The words so impressed him that he wrote a tune for them, called "Olivet."

A few days later the two met again. Dr. Mason said to Mr. Palmer, "You may live many years and do many things, but I think you will be best known to posterity as the author of this song." Dr. Mason was not far wrong.

> **May Thy rich grace impart**
> **Strength to my fainting heart,**
> **My zeal inspire;**
> **As Thou hast died for me,**
> **Oh, may my love to Thee**
> **Pure, warm, and changeless be,**
> **A living fire!**

Now I skip to the fourth verse:

> **When ends life's transient dream,**
> **When death's cold, sullen stream**
> **Shall o'er me roll,**
> **Blest Saviour, then, in love,**
> **Fear and distrust remove;**
> **Oh, bear me safe above,**
> **A ransomed soul!**

Your experiences with the Lord may not result in the writing of a famous hymn, but they can and should be very worthwhile and very dear to you. Treasure these experiences and seek out times and places where you may be alone with the Lord.

Reflection: Ray Palmer's faith was not in himself or some "higher power," but in Christ. Our faith also must be in Him. The Bible says that Christ "was in all points tempted like as we are, yet [He was] without sin" (Heb. 4:15). In every situation that we find ourselves in, remember, Christ has been there too.

Assurance

It Is Well With My Soul

Isaiah 48:10–22

"O that thou hadst hearkened to my commandments! then had thy peace been as a river, and thy righteousness as the waves of the sea."—Vs. 18.

Horatio G. Spafford was a successful businessman in Chicago with a wife and five children. The Spaffords were not strangers to sorrow and tragedy. They had lost an infant son in death, and much of their business in the great Chicago fire. Yet they had learned that God was in control of every aspect of their lives. The Lord blessed them by allowing the business to flourish again and by giving them more children.

On November 21, 1873, the French ocean liner *Ville de Havre* was crossing the Atlantic from the United States to Europe. On board were Mrs. Spafford and four of the children, all looking forward to a wonderful holiday. Mr. Spafford had stayed home to care for some unexpected business problem but intended to join the family in a few days.

About four days into the crossing of the Atlantic, the *Ville de Havre* collided with a powerful, iron-hulled English ship, the *Loch Eme*. Mrs. Spafford, her four children and the 221 other passengers were in grave danger. Mrs. Spafford hurriedly brought the four children to the deck, knelt with them and prayed that God would spare them if that could be His will or make them willing to endure whatever awaited them. (It is reported that the children had become Christians just two weeks before.)

Within a matter of minutes the ship slipped beneath the dark waters of the Atlantic, carrying with it most of the passengers, including the Spafford children. A sailor was rowing over the spot where the ship had sunk when he spotted a woman floating on a piece of the wreckage—Mrs.

Spafford. He pulled her into the boat, and they were picked up by another ship which landed them in Cardiff, Wales, nine days later. From there she wired her husband this message: SAVED, ALONE. (Mr. Spafford later framed the telegram and hung it in his office.)

Spafford booked passage on the next available ship to join his heartbroken wife. With the ship about four days out, the captain told him that as far as they could determine, they were near the spot where the ship had gone down with his children.

It is reported that Spafford went to his cabin to rest but could not. He, in his assurance that God is always good, wrote "It Is Well With My Soul."

First stanza:

When peace, like a river, attendeth my way,
  When sorrows like sea billows roll,
Whatever my lot, Thou hast taught me to say,
  It is well, it is well with my soul.

Chorus:

  It is well with my soul;
  It is well, it is well with my soul.

Fourth stanza:

And, Lord, haste the day when my faith shall be sight,
  The clouds be rolled back as a scroll.
The trump shall resound, and the Lord shall descend;
  "Even so"—it is well with my soul.

Spafford later carried his poem to a brilliant young song-writer, Philip P. Bliss, who wrote a moving musical setting that has carried the song around the world. Bliss himself met tragedy, when at age thirty-eight he died in a horrible train wreck.

In 1881 Spafford and his wife moved to Jerusalem where

they helped build an American colony. There they lived for the remainder of their lives.

Reflection: God gives us His peace when we meet His requirements. Many times He sends unusual circumstances into our lives to make us more like His Son. If all things are accepted as from Him, then His peace is the result.

Blessed Thoughts of Heaven

Shall We Gather at the River?

Revelation 22:1–7
"And he shewed me a pure river of water of life, clear as crystal, proceeding out of the throne of God and of the Lamb."—Vs. 1.

Many of the hymn writers of the past have written hymns at will or have created a mood in which to write, as did Fanny Crosby. Not so with Robert Lowry. He waited for a mood to come upon him before writing.

Lowry entered the ministry upon graduation from Bucknell University in 1854, holding pastorates in New York, Pennsylvania and New Jersey. It was while he was a pastor at the Hansen Place Baptist Church in Brooklyn that he wrote "Shall We Gather at the River?"

On a sultry day in July 1864, Robert Lowry threw himself on a lounge in his home in a state of exhaustion. As he fell to thinking of future things, of the gathering of the saints around God's throne, he began to wonder why so many of the hymn writers had written so much of the "river of death" and so little of the "river of life."

A hymn began to take form, first as a question, "Shall we gather at the river?" Then came the answer, "Yes, we'll gather at the river." Soon the words and music were completed.

It is so much a favorite among Christians, you find it in almost every hymnal.

Robert Lowry was responsible for one of his church member's becoming a famous hymn writer—Annie Sherwood Hawks, who wrote "I Need Thee Every Hour." He composed the music for her hymn. He was a kind, generous man who did all he could to encourage others to make the most of their talents.

Shall we gather at the river

8

> Where bright angel feet have trod,
> With its crystal tide forever
> Flowing by the throne of God?

Verse four:

> Soon we'll reach the shining river;
> Soon our pilgrimage will cease;
> Soon our happy hearts will quiver
> With the melody of peace.

Chorus:

> Yes, we'll gather at the river,
> The beautiful, the beautiful river,
> Gather with the saints at the river
> That flows by the throne of God.

Reflection: As Robert Lowry did, you and I should find it refreshing to ponder our heavenly Home, with all its beauty and wonder; better yet, to ponder going there one day.

Blind Faith?

All the Way My Saviour Leads Me

Philippians 4:6–23

"But my God shall supply all your need according to his riches in glory by Christ Jesus."—Vs. 19.

Those who knew Fanny Crosby may have heard her many times over greet her friends with, "God bless your dear soul."

Even though she was blind from six weeks on, she lived a life of cheerfulness. Once she declared that, on the whole, it had been good that she had been blind. Of the loss of her sight, she said she felt the Lord didn't order it, but could see why He permitted it to happen. A favorite text was, "What I do thou knowest not now; but thou shalt know hereafter." She often quoted:

> **His purposes will ripen fast,**
> **Unfolding every hour;**
> **The bud may have a bitter taste,**
> **But sweet will be the flower.**

By her ninety-fourth year, she had written eight thousand Christian songs and hymns and had scattered sunshine and happiness wherever she went.

On one occasion she needed a small amount of cash. Not having time to contact her publishers to ask for an advance, she knelt in prayer, asking God to supply her need. Then she arose and began to walk back and forth in her room, trying to get into a mood to write another hymn. (She was under contract with her publishers to write three hymns each week.)

Suddenly—a knock at the door! She greeted her visitor with her usual, "God bless your dear soul." After a few minutes of visiting with her, the guest arose and started to leave. In bidding her good-bye, he shook her hand and left in it the exact amount she needed.

Immediately she knelt again, this time to thank God for answering her prayer. She arose, her heart bubbling with joy, and was inspired to write "All the Way My Saviour Leads Me." The first stanza says:

> **All the way my Saviour leads me;**
> **What have I to ask beside?**
> **Can I doubt His tender mercy,**
> **Who through life has been my Guide?**
> **Heav'nly peace, divinest comfort,**
> **Here by faith in Him to dwell!**
> **For I know, whate'er befall me,**
> **Jesus doeth all things well.**

Reflection: God knows our needs and will supply them if we trust Him. He sends the times of want so that we may enjoy the times of plenty. He sends the clouds so that we can better appreciate the sunshine. He sends us into the valley so we may recognize His mountain peaks of rich blessings.

Bound With Strong Cords

Blest Be the Tie That Binds

Galatians 6:1–10

"And let us not be weary in well doing: for in due season we shall reap, if we faint not. As we have therefore opportunity, let us do good unto all men, especially unto them who are of the household of faith."—Vss. 9, 10.

John Fawcett had been pastor of a small church at Wainsgate in Yorkshire, England, for seven years. His income was small, and his family was growing much too large to be supported by his meager wages. It seemed only practical to move to a church that paid a larger salary; so when a call came, it was accepted.

Moving day arrived. The men were loading the preacher's furniture and books on the wagons. The last piece loaded, everything seemed set for the journey. Men, women and children stood around the wagons weeping over the loss of their beloved pastor.

Seated on packed cases, the pastor and his wife could not restrain their tears. They and the church members were remembering the times when he had stood with a weeping family from whom the Lord had taken a loved one, or with a young husband anxiously awaiting the arrival of his firstborn. Perhaps still fresh in their minds were the times when he had taken his Bible and, quietly and earnestly, shown the way of salvation to a lost one; or perhaps the times when he had preached in the little church and the Holy Spirit had visited them in a special way. All of these things could not be brushed from their minds, nor did they want them to be.

Finally, Mrs. Fawcett turned to her husband and tearfully told him that she did not know how they could go. He confessed that he had the same feelings.

He gave orders to unload the wagons and put everything

back in its place. Out of genuine Christian love for his people, the preacher stayed and ministered to their needs for fifty years.

The incidents which occurred on the day he almost moved, coupled with the spirit of those kind people at Wainsgate, inspired him to write "Blest Be the Tie That Binds."

> **Blest be the tie that binds**
> **Our hearts in Christian love;**
> **The fellowship of kindred minds**
> **Is like to that above.**
>
> **Before our Father's throne,**
> **We pour our ardent prayers;**
> **Our fears, our hopes, our aims are one,**
> **Our comforts and our cares.**

Now verse four:

> **When we asunder part,**
> **It gives us inward pain,**
> **But we shall still be joined in heart**
> **And hope to meet again.**

John Fawcett passed away in 1817 after a life of service to God's people that spanned seventy-seven years.

Reflection: Thank God for you pastors who labor so tirelessly among humble people, with little recompense save the knowledge that God sees you, guides you and will supply your every need.

May God give each of us the ability to stay with the task until it is finished.

The Cabinetmaker's Song

The Solid Rock

Matthew 7:24–29

"Therefore whosoever heareth these sayings of mine, and doeth them, I will liken him unto a wise man, which built his house upon a rock."—Vs. 24.

Edward Mote wrote only one song, but what a song! It has blessed Christians around the world.

He rose from an unruly childhood to become a great writer and preacher. He said of his youth, "My Sundays were spent on the streets [of London] in play. So ignorant was I, I did not know there was a God."

As he grew older, he attended Tottenham Court Road Chapel where he heard sermons by the noted preacher, John Hyatt. He soon found that Jesus Christ could take away all the fears of life and give him the peace of heart and mind that he had long desired.

He became a carpenter apprentice and, through hard labor and conscientious efforts, came to own his own cabinet shop. One day while walking to his work, he began thinking that he should write a hymn. Before he reached his shop, he had the chorus: "On Christ, the solid Rock, I stand; all other ground is sinking sand." Before the day ended, he had written four stanzas.

The following Sunday he visited in the home of a preacher friend whose wife was at the point of death. During the afternoon they read from the Scriptures and had prayer with her. Then as the preacher looked for a hymnal from which to sing (as was his custom), he could find none. Mr. Mote reached into his pocket and pulled out his verses and asked if he could sing them to her.

Seeing how much comfort she found in listening to the verses, Mr. Mote had one thousand copies printed for distribution among his friends.

Some time later Edward Mote became a Baptist preacher. His efforts made it possible for a house of worship to be built for his congregation. They were so grateful that they offered to deed the property to him, but he replied, "I do not want the chapel; I want only the pulpit; and when I cease to preach Christ, then turn me out of that."

He served this congregation for more than twenty years, never missing a single Lord's Day.

In his seventy-seventh year, as he lay on his bed of sickness, he replied, "I think I am going to Heaven—yes, I am nearing port. The truths I have preached I am now living upon, and they will do to die upon. Ah! The precious blood which takes away all our sins! It is this which makes peace with God."

What a victorious ending of a useful life! He was reared in a godless home, learned an honorable trade, then gave it up to become a preacher. His memory will remain for generations because he took time one day to write the song, "The Solid Rock."

> **My hope is built on nothing less**
> **Than Jesus' blood and righteousness;**
> **I dare not trust the sweetest frame,**
> **But wholly lean on Jesus' name.**

Chorus:

> **On Christ, the solid Rock, I stand;**
> **All other ground is sinking sand,**
> **All other ground is sinking sand.**

There are four stanzas to the song.

Reflection: God needs men and women who are willing to serve Him in whatever capacity He may deem necessary. It is our solemn duty as sincere Christians to rest on "The Solid Rock" and be obedient.

Capturing Peace During Sorrow

I Heard the Bells on Christmas Day

Luke 2:1–20
"Glory to God in the highest, and on earth peace, good will toward men."—Vs. 14.

Tragedy struck the home of America's most popular poet. On July 9, 1861, Henry Wadsworth Longfellow's wife, Fanny, was near an open window sealing locks of her daughter's hair in a packet, using hot sealing wax. It was never known whether a spark from a match or the sealing wax was the cause, but suddenly her dress caught fire and engulfed her with flames. Her husband, sleeping in the next room, was awakened by her screams. He was severely burned on his face and hands as he tried desperately to put out the fire and save his wife.

Tragically burned, she slipped into a coma the next day and died. His grievous burns would not even allow him to attend her funeral.

He seemed to lock the anguish within his soul. Because he continued to work at his craft, only his family knew of his personal suffering. They could see it in his eyes and observe his long periods of silence. His white beard, so identified with him, was one of the results of the tragedy—the burn scars on his face made shaving almost impossible.

Although a legend in his own time, he still needed the peace that God gives to His children. On Christmas Day, three years following the horrible accident (at age fifty-seven), he sat down to try to capture, if possible, the joys of the season. He began to write:

> **I heard the bells on Christmas Day**
> **Their old familiar carols play**
> **And wild and sweet the words repeat**
> **Of peace on earth, good will to men.**

16

As he came to the third stanza, he was stopped by the thought of the condition of his beloved country. The Civil War was in full swing. The Battle of Gettysburg was not long past. Days looked dark, and he probably asked himself, *How can I write about 'peace on earth, good will to men' in this war-torn country, where brother fights against brother, and father against son?* But he kept writing. And what did he write?

> **And in despair I bowed my head:**
> **"There is no peace on earth," I said,**
> **"For hate is strong and mocks the song**
> **Of peace on earth, good will to men."**

It seems as if he could have been writing for our day. Then, as all of us should do, he turned his thoughts to the One who solves all problems, the One who can give true and perfect peace. He continued writing:

> **Then pealed the bells more loud and deep:**
> **"God is not dead, nor doth He sleep;**
> **The wrong shall fail, the right prevail,**
> **With peace on earth, good will to men."**

And so we have the marvelous carol, "I Heard the Bells on Christmas Day." A musician named J. Baptiste Calkin wrote the musical setting that has helped make the carol a favorite.

Reflection: Just as that Christmas in 1864 was made better for Longfellow, you too can experience great happiness. You can actually find the true peace with God that Longfellow wrote about in the carol. As you pillow your head tonight, you can know that you are God's child. You can know for sure that you have a home in Heaven, prepared just for you.

The Children Love the Bachelor

O Little Town of Bethlehem

Matthew 2:1–15

"And thou Bethlehem, in the land of Juda, art not the least among the princes of Juda: for out of thee shall come a Governor, that shall rule my people Israel."—Vs. 6.

"O Mother, how happy the angels will be!" was the startling yet tender comment of a child, a member of the church where Phillips Brooks was pastor, when she heard of his passing on to Heaven.

There is an old adage: "His hat may be greasy, and his trousers may not be creased; but if his children flatten their noses against the windowpane thirty minutes before he comes home from work, you can trust him with anything you have."

Phillips Brooks had no children of his own—in fact, he was never married—but he loved the children of his congregations very dearly, and they returned the affection.

It is reported that he had a toy box in the corner of his office for the girls and boys who came by. He was never too busy to play dolls with the little girls or scuffle with the boys. To them he must have been a gentle giant.

It was under his ministry that the Holy Trinity Church of Boston became such a renowned lighthouse. Unlike most Episcopals of his day, he preached the evangelical Gospel of Jesus Christ. He was six-and-a-half feet tall and, from all I can gather, possessed the kindness of a Washington, the poise of a Lincoln, the fire of a Sunday and the delivery of a Bryan.

In 1865 he was granted a leave of absence from his church in Philadelphia to visit the Holy Land. He saw the place of the shepherds and joined in the traditional services on Christmas Eve at the Church of the Nativity. This was such a memorable experience for him that he later wrote a poem for the children of his Sunday school.

The next day he gave the poem to Lewis Redner, the organist and Sunday school superintendent, and asked him to set it to music.

On Saturday, the night before Christmas, Redner still had not come up with the music. During the night he awakened with a new tune ringing in his ears. He quickly jotted down the notes and promptly went back to sleep. He arose early the next morning and wrote the harmony for the new song in time for the children to sing it at Sunday school.

"O Little Town of Bethlehem" remained relatively unknown for about twenty years, then it was published in an Episcopal hymnal. From that time its popularity has spread until now at the Christmas season people everywhere sing:

> **O little town of Bethlehem,**
> **How still we see thee lie!**
> **Above thy deep and dreamless sleep**
> **The silent stars go by.**
> **Yet in thy dark streets shineth**
> **The everlasting Light;**
> **The hopes and fears of all the years**
> **Are met in thee tonight.**
>
> **For Christ is born of Mary,**
> **And gathered all above,**
> **While mortals sleep, the angels keep**
> **Their watch of wond'ring love.**
> **O morning stars, together**
> **Proclaim the holy birth**
> **And praises sing to God the King**
> **And peace to men on earth.**

The other stanzas tell more of "our Lord Emmanuel."

Reflection: Children loved Phillips Brooks because he loved them and took time from his busy schedule to make sure that they shared in one of the most memorable occasions of his lifetime. Not only did he share this occasion with *them,* but he shares it with *us* also.

A Church Mouse Moved
the Show

Silent Night! Holy Night!

Luke 2:1–12

"For unto you is born this day in the city of David a Saviour, which is Christ the Lord."—Vs. 11.

In 1818 a band of roving actors appeared in the village of Oberndorf, near Salzburg, a small town in the Austrian Alps. The showmen were there for the annual presentation of the Christmas story to be held at St. Nicholas Church. But the organ was rendered unplayable by a church mouse that had eaten a hole in the bellows. It could not be repaired in time for the performance, so the simple show was presented in a private home.

The assistant pastor, Josef Mohr, was invited to attend. So impressed was he with the play and the sincerity of the actors that, as he walked home that evening, he began to reflect on the real meaning of the Christmas story.

As Mohr strode to a hillside overlooking the village as it lay shrouded in a still, clear night, the silence of the snowy hillsides reminded him of a special silent night over eighteen hundred years before. When he reached his home, he penned the words to a poem and titled it "Silent Night! Holy Night!" Later he showed the verses to the church organist, Franz Gruber, a schoolmaster and songwriter. It is reported that Gruber composed a musical setting the same day he received the poem from Mohr.

A few days later, during a Christmas Eve service, Gruber and Mohr sang the song to the small congregation gathered in the church. The organ was still in ill repair, forcing Gruber to accompany them on his guitar.

A few weeks later the organ repairman finally made it to Oberndorf. As he finished his repair work, Gruber slid onto the organ bench and began to play. It is reported that he played "Silent Night! Holy Night!" The repairman was so impressed with this new song that he took it back to his village.

This carol was a favorite from the beginning. Soon the Strasser Sisters, Austrian concert singers, began singing it throughout Europe. From there it has orbited the earth again and again. It was translated by Jane Campbell into English from the Austrian language in 1863 and made its first appearance in America in 1871 in Charles Hutchins's *Sunday School Hymnal.*

> **Silent night, holy night,**
> **All is calm, all is bright**
> **Round yon virgin mother and Child.**
> **Holy Infant, so tender and mild,**
> **Sleep in heavenly peace,**
> **Sleep in heavenly peace.**

"Silent Night! Holy Night!" is one of those carols that wears like steel. It is as fresh and beautiful today as it was the first time it was sung in the little Austrian town more than 170 years ago, and is probably the most widely known carol in the world. It has been translated into scores of languages.

Wouldn't it be wonderful if we could experience something akin to this "heavenly peace" of the last line? As you sing this carol during the holiday season, remember to pray for peace in our world.

Reflection: Pause a few moments and be thankful for this gift of love from God the Father, who sent His only Son to be our Saviour. Then, for you too it will be a silent, holy night.

Confrontation

Come Thou Fount

I John 1

"If we confess our sins, he is faithful and just to forgive us our sins, and to cleanse us from all unrighteousness."—Vs. 9.

How sad for a young boy to have to grow up without a dad. Robert Robinson's dad passed away when Robert was only eight years of age. As soon as he was old enough, he got a job as an apprentice to a barber. Because of the hardship of having to be the breadwinner for his widowed mother and himself, his formal education was limited. However, his knowledge was varied and extensive because he spent many hours in study.

Robert Robinson was born in Norfolk, England, in September 1735. As he grew older, he came under the influence of that great evangelist, George Whitefield. He became convicted of his terrible, sinful ways. On December 10, 1755, Robinson could not escape from a particular phrase used by Mr. Whitefield in one of his sermons: "O my hearers! The wrath to come! The wrath to come!"

He was wonderfully converted and became a minister of the Gospel, first in a Baptist church, then in a Methodist church and later in other denominations. Then, unfortunately, he became altogether unstable and unhappy. Some would call it backslidden.

He found himself one day the fellow passenger of a young lady on a stagecoach. It is reported that she began to sing to break the monotony of the trip. And what did she sing?

> **Come, Thou Fount of ev'ry blessing,**
> **Tune my heart to sing Thy grace;**
> **Streams of mercy, never ceasing,**
> **Call for songs of loudest praise.**

> **Teach me some melodious sonnet,**
> **Sung by flaming tongues above;**
> **Praise the mount—I'm fixed upon it,**
> **Mount of Thy redeeming love.**

The last stanza reads:

> **Oh, to grace how great a debtor**
> **Daily I'm constrained to be!**
> **Let Thy goodness, like a fetter,**
> **Bind my wand'ring heart to Thee.**
> **Prone to wander, Lord, I feel it,**
> **Prone to leave the God I love.**
> **Here's my heart, oh, take and seal it;**
> **Seal it for Thy courts above.**

She asked him what he thought about the song, and his startling reply was: "Madam, I am the unhappy man who wrote that hymn many years ago, and I would give a thousand worlds, if I had them, to feel now as I felt then."

Reflection: During each day, may you never stray farther from the Lord than His fingertips, and every evening may you draw close to His heart!

A Constant Companion

God Be With You Till We Meet Again

II Corinthians 13:5–11

"Finally, brethren, farewell. Be perfect, be of good comfort, be of one mind, live in peace; and the God of love and peace shall be with you."—Vs. 11.

The etymology of the word *good-bye* is a condensation of the words "God be with ye."

Dr. J. E. Rankin, former pastor of the First Congregational Church in Washington, felt the need of a song for Christians to sing as a farewell to one another. He fell to thinking of the term *good-bye* and, upon learning of its origin, began to write a poem:

> **God be with you till we meet again,**
> **By His counsels guide, uphold you,**
> **With His sheep securely fold you;**
> **God be with you till we meet again.**

After he finished the first stanza, he sent it to two music composers—one a famous, well-trained musician, and the other an obscure choir director. Both submitted music, and the melody of the latter seemed to fit the verse perfectly.

While a student at Tennessee Temple Schools in Chattanooga, Tennessee, I had the rare privilege of helping to send off missionaries who had graduated and were ready to do the work to which God had called them.

At the train depot there were always mixed emotions: some were crying; some, smiling; some, just standing quietly. All were caught up in the solemnity of the occasion. A student who had successfully completed his course of study was now ready to go out and face the trials and hardships of the mission field. Leaving friends, family and home seemed to fade into insignificance as the young volunteers anticipated the joys that come from obeying God.

25

As the conductor called, "B-o-o-o-a-r-d!" a lump came into many throats, but the well-wishers sang as best they could. As the train slipped from sight, you could hear above the click of the wheels:

> **God be with you till we meet again,**
> **Keep love's banner floating o'er you,**
> **Smite death's threatening wave before you;**
> **God be with you till we meet again.**

Reflection: If we strengthen ourselves with the study of the Bible, we will be able, in a convincing manner, to impart to others this living truth: God will be with you wherever His providence may take you.

Do It Again, Lord!

Break Thou the Bread of Life

John 6:29–40
"For the bread of God is he which cometh down from heaven, and giveth life unto the world."—Vs. 33.

One morning a small lad left home with five barley loaves and two fishes. During the course of the day he and his food became a significant part of one of the best-known miracles Jesus ever performed—the feeding of the five thousand.

Later, the scriptural account of this glorious miracle gave rise to a much-loved gospel song written by Mary Artemisia Lathbury.

Dr. John Vincent (later Bishop Vincent of the Methodist Church) instituted the Chautauqua Assembly, a Methodist camp meeting grounds on Lake Chautauqua in New York. One facet of the Chautauqua Assembly was the Chautauqua Literary and Scientific Circle.

During the encampment of 1877, Dr. Vincent asked Miss Lathbury to write a song that could be used as a study song during the sessions. The result was the beautiful and ever popular "Break Thou the Bread of Life," which is included in almost every hymnal today.

> **Break Thou the bread of life,**
> > **Dear Lord, to me,**
> **As Thou didst break the loaves**
> > **Beside the sea.**
> **Beyond the sacred page**
> > **I seek Thee, Lord;**
> **My spirit pants for Thee,**
> > **O living Word.**
>
> **Bless Thou the truth, dear Lord,**
> > **To me, to me,**

As Thou didst bless the bread
    By Galilee;
Then shall all bondage cease,
    All fetters fall,
And I shall find my peace,
    My All in All.

Thou art the Bread of Life,
    O Lord, to me;
Thy holy Word, the truth
    That saveth me.
Give me to eat and live
    With Thee above;
Teach me to love Thy truth,
    For Thou art love.

Oh, send Thy Spirit, Lord,
    Now unto me,
That He may touch my eyes
    And make me see;
Show me the truth concealed
    Within Thy Word,
And in Thy Book revealed
    I see the Lord.

Reflection: We are blessed indeed when we feed our souls with the "Bread of God." When Jesus, through a lad, shared with thousands, He was giving us a valuable lesson: sharing Christ with others. Many are famishing in a world of spiritual hunger. Let us do what we can to help.

The Dreamer

Throw Out the Lifeline

Daniel 12:2–13

"And they that be wise shall shine as the brightness of the firmament; and they that turn many to righteousness as the stars for ever and ever."—Vs. 3.

During the latter years of the nineteenth century, the remains of several destroyed ships could be seen clearly at low tide a little offshore from Westwood, a small seacoast town near Boston, Massachusetts. A Baptist pastor, Edwin S. Ufford, liked to stroll along the seashore and look out to sea. In his mind's eye he could see the panic-stricken victims as they desperately strove for life itself. "I could see a storm, a spar, a shipwrecked sailor drifting out beyond human reach," he said.

Later he visited several life-saving stations and watched men practice rescue techniques that all too often were needed along that rocky coast. He heard the leader bark out the order: "Throw out the lifeline!" He was shown the lifeline.

Several men recounted dramatic rescues in which the lifeline was used. Those impressions, coupled with the scenes of rotting boat hulls, produced the hymn "Throw Out the Lifeline." In fifteen minutes, Mr. Ufford wrote these memorable words:

> **Throw out the lifeline across the dark wave;**
> **There is a brother whom someone should save.**
> **Somebody's brother! oh, who then will dare**
> **To throw out the lifeline, his peril to share?**

Chorus:

> **Throw out the lifeline!**
> **Throw out the lifeline!**
> **Someone is drifting away.**
> **Throw out the lifeline!**

29

Throw out the lifeline!
Someone is sinking today.

There is an urgency in the other stanzas to win souls while we can, for soon the season of rescue will be over.

An interesting sequel to the story is that several years later Mr. Ufford was invited to a religious service in California to tell the story of this hymn. He was able to carry with him a real visual aid for the audience—a piece of the lifeline used when the *Elsie Smith* sank off Cape Cod in 1902. After the meeting, a survivor from the *Elsie Smith* identified himself as being one of those who had been saved by that very lifeline.

Reflection: Your greatest need is to become a rescuer after you have been rescued, to tell someone else the Good News after you have become a Christian. All about you are those who need to hear of Jesus and His love.

Freedom's Holy Light

My Country, 'Tis of Thee

John 8:31–36

"If the Son therefore shall make you free, ye shall be free indeed."—Vs. 36.

What a thrill it was for Samuel Francis Smith as he stood in Boston on July 4, 1832, and heard a children's choir at one of the city's churches sing a song he had written.

Five months earlier, Smith, a seminary student, had been sitting in his room on the campus that was not very far from the church in which the lantern was hung during Paul Revere's famous ride. Lowell Mason, a music publisher, had given young Smith, who spoke several languages, a number of European music books, thinking that he might translate some of the songs for a new hymnal. Smith's eyes fell on a German song entitled "God Bless Our Native Land." (The tune had already been used in England for more than a hundred years as "God Save the King.")

Instead of translating the original song, Samuel decided to write new words for the tune. Just thirty minutes before sundown, he picked up a small piece of paper and, as the sun was setting, wrote the last line of what was to become one of the most famous of our country's songs. He later declared that he had not intentionally tried to write a patriotic song, but it soon became so popular that it almost became our national anthem.

Later, Samuel Francis Smith became a Baptist preacher and went on to author several books, teach languages, hold a number of positions within his denomination and write 150 hymns, the most famous of which is a missionary song, "The Morning Light Is Breaking."

During his eighty-eighth year, Smith passed away at a train station as he was about to board. During his long and useful life, he was a blessing and inspiration to multitudes of people—and he left to you and me "My Country, 'Tis of Thee." Here are stanzas one and four:

> **My country, 'tis of thee,**
> **Sweet land of liberty,**
> > **Of thee I sing;**
> **Land where my fathers died,**
> **Land of the pilgrim's pride,**
> **From ev'ry mountainside**
> > **Let freedom ring!**

> **Our fathers' God, to Thee,**
> **Author of liberty,**
> > **To Thee we sing;**
> **Long may our land be bright**
> **With freedom's holy light;**
> **Protect us by Thy might,**
> > **Great God, our King!**

In our day, when freedom and life in the United States are so cherished, scarcely a person old enough to sing does not know Samuel Smith's masterpiece. Each time it is heard, we should thank our Heavenly Father for all the blessings that we enjoy as Americans. Sing it bravely. Sing it proudly. And I repeat, sing it with gratitude in your heart.

The tune was titled "America" (and sometimes the song is called by that name), but we more often and perhaps more correctly call it "My Country, 'Tis of Thee."

Reflection: One of the foremost blessings you and I enjoy from God's hand is the freedom to live in America, "sweet land of liberty." Yet our most cherished freedom is available to all God's children—the liberation from the bondage of sin.

From Heartache to Assurance

No One Ever Cared for Me Like Jesus

I Peter 5:1–7

"Casting all your care upon him; for he careth for you."— Vs. 7.

"LET 'ER RIP!" was an expression of one of America's foremost gospel songwriters, Dr. Charles F. Weigle. This little expression, odd as it may seem, simply suggests that one should not worry about situations over which he has little or no control, but leave them in the hands of God. This godly attitude allowed Dr. Weigle to be a blessing and inspiration to countless thousands during his fruitful life. His booklet called *Quit Worrying* has helped many with their anxiety problems.

I had the privilege of knowing Dr. Weigle personally and even had the opportunity to direct the music in one of his revival campaigns. I was a young song leader, and he was an elderly evangelist in his eighties. He lived on the campus of Tennessee Temple University during his last years. As a student, I got to fellowship with him on campus, often sharing meals with him in the dining commons.

Charles Frederick Weigle was born in Lafayette, Indiana on November 20, 1871. He was converted at the age of twelve. With the help of Christian friends and an unswerving faith in God, he became a true and faithful laborer for Jesus Christ. Later, he felt the call of God and surrendered to preach the Gospel. His life of service to God was enhanced greatly by his ability to write gospel songs.

Dr. Weigle was not without his hours of trouble and heartache. Yet it seems that out of these grievous sorrows flowed forth one of the most beautiful and widely known of his songs, "No One Ever Cared for Me Like Jesus." Phil Kerr, a religious broadcaster on the West Coast, reported that requests for it outnumbered requests for any other

33

special gospel song. It has been sung around the world and translated into many languages.

One day Dr. Weigle came home to find a note from his wife declaring that she was leaving and going to the "world" to get the things that she felt were owed to her. She no longer wanted to be the wife of an evangelist.

This situation threw him into such a state of depression that he actually thought of ending his life. As he was wondering if anyone cared, he heard a small voice within saying, "Charlie, I haven't forgotten you. I still care for you."

At this, he fell to his knees asking God to forgive him for not trusting Him completely and determined never again to let such a thought cross his mind.

In less than five years his wife was dead. While reflecting on the past experiences and the goodness of God who carried him through the heartache, he once again felt the urge to write a song. The song would be a summation of his whole life's experience with his wonderful Lord. He later said that "the lyric came as fast as I could put it down." It was the first song he had written since his world fell apart. Now, he wanted everyone to know that "No One Ever Cared for Me Like Jesus."

Many stories could be written about the songs of Charles Weigle. He wrote several hundred in all, and many became greatly beloved among multitudes of Christians.

Reflection: How often have you wondered, *Does anyone really care?* Well, there is One who loves you and cares for you more than you care for yourself. Turn every problem over to Him...right now!

From Rags to Riches

Then Jesus Came

Mark 10:43-52

"And Jesus said unto him, Go thy way; thy faith hath made thee whole. And immediately he received his sight, and followed Jesus in the way."—Vs. 52.

In the late 1930s a number of individuals had a part in the writing of one of our most stirring evangelistic songs. In a large meeting in the Billy Sunday Tabernacle at the Winona Lake Bible Conference Grounds in Winona Lake, Indiana, Mr. Homer Rodeheaver, Billy Sunday's song leader, heard a sermon by Evangelist Mel Trotter in which he vividly described his conversion experience, how God had lifted him from a horrible pit of drunkenness and near suicide.

As Trotter walked along Clark Street one night in Chicago contemplating suicide, someone urged him to go into the Pacific Garden Mission. There he found Christ, who changed his life completely and forever.

In describing how low he had sunk, Trotter told his audience that before he met Christ, he had stolen the new shoes off the feet of his little daughter who had died and was awaiting burial, and sold them for a few pennies to buy another drink.

He convincingly told his audience how Christ changed his life after he became a Christian. As he gave the altar call following his sermon, many responded. It was a message and an illustration that lingered in the minds of all who heard him.

After the service, a number of people gathered for food and fellowship in the home of Homer Rodeheaver, who lived only a short distance away. Their conversation was about the service they had just attended and the sermon they had just heard. Dr. Harry Rimmer, one of Rodeheaver's guests, remarked how everything changes when

Jesus comes into our lives. The situation and the remarks by Dr. Rimmer started Rodeheaver to thinking that someone should write a song expressing those very truths. It all kept ringing in his mind.

A few days later he traveled to Philadelphia to a branch office of his music publishing company. While there, he was visited by Dr. Oswald Smith, pastor of the great People's Church of Toronto, Canada, a mighty supporter of foreign missions and a wonderful songwriter. He was in the city for some speaking engagements and came into the offices. Rodeheaver told him of the recent service and his thoughts about the changing power of Christ and asked him if he would try writing a suitable poem that he might set to music.

Dr. Smith went back to his room and, before the day was done, returned with a poem entitled "Then Jesus Came."

A melody came quickly to Rodeheaver, who passed the whole project along to his music editor, C. Austin Miles, composer of "In the Garden." Miles put the song on manuscript paper, and Rodeheaver sang it at a meeting that very evening.

Reflection: When Christ comes into a life, He sets the captive free. "Old things are passed away; behold, all things are become new."

Give Me All in This House

Take My Life, and Let It Be

Romans 12:1–16

"I beseech you therefore, brethren, by the mercies of God, that ye present your bodies a living sacrifice, holy, acceptable unto God, which is your reasonable service."— Vs. 1.

"Splendid! to be so near the gates of Heaven" were farewell words of the short but useful life of Frances Ridley Havergal.

Miss Havergal was born in Ashley, Worcestershire, in 1836. She showed an aptitude for poetry when she was only seven. She later trained in music, becoming proficient in playing the piano. She was very healthy and strong in her younger years, but in her early twenties she became ill and was confined to a wheelchair most of the rest of her life. Even in those trying years, she kept a cheerful attitude and was able to be a blessing to those with whom she came in contact. It is reported that she never once complained of her infirmities.

One of her most popular songs came as a result of a five-day visit to London. Several of the ten members of that household were unconverted, while others were not rejoicing Christians. She asked God to give her all in the house before she left.

On the last night of her stay, the governess took her to see the two daughters, who were weeping. They were both deeply concerned about their spiritual welfare and were asking to see Miss Havergal. She led them to Christ, making the family circle complete.

Miss Havergal later confessed that she stayed up most of the night rejoicing and reconsecrating her own life to God. As the hours with God wore on, the lines of a poem began to form in her mind. They came in couplets, something like this:

Take my life, and let it be
Consecrated, Lord, to Thee.

Take my moments and my days;
Let them flow in ceaseless praise.

Take my hands and let them move
At the impulse of Thy love.

This hymn, coming out of a period of great devotion in her life, is probably our greatest song of consecration.

Take my will and make it Thine;
It shall be no longer mine.
Take my heart, it is Thine own;
It shall be Thy royal throne,
It shall be Thy royal throne.

Take my love, my God, I pour
At Thy feet its treasure store;
Take myself, and I will be
Ever, only, all for Thee,
Ever, only, all for Thee.

Reflection: How refreshing to read of one so infirm that she was confined to a wheelchair, yet whose thoughts were continually on others. Whatever your condition, it can be made brighter and more cheerful if your thoughts are turned to others. Live in such a way that in your sunset years, you can look back and see someone was helped, some life was made better, because of you.

God Hid a Song in His Heart

I *Surrender All*

Romans 12:1–15; Philippians 3:7–14

"But what things were gain to me, those I counted loss for Christ."—Phil. 3:7.

One of the most widely used songs in Christendom and its composer are the subjects of this story. It is probably one of the most oft-used invitation songs in churches across the United States and many other countries, ranking in popularity with "Just As I Am" and "Have Thine Own Way."

Our songwriter, Dr. Judson W. Van DeVenter, was born in Monroe County, Michigan on December 5, 1855. He was educated in the public schools of Dundee, Michigan and at Hillsdale College, also in Michigan, graduating in 1875. He became a Christian at age seventeen and joined the Methodist Church. As he grew older he studied drawing and painting under a well-known German teacher. He said, "To help me financially, I taught school and eventually became supervisor of art in the public schools of Sharon, Pennsylvania."

Dr. Al Smith in his book *Hymn Histories* quotes him as saying, "It was during this period (teaching art in the public schools) that a revival was held in the First United Methodist Church of which I was a member." Van DeVenter was a personal worker in the meetings and became extremely involved in the services.

Not long after that revival effort he was licensed as a lay preacher. The Lord blessed his efforts, and he saw many souls born into the family of God. He felt a strong urge from the Lord to give up his teaching and enter the field of evangelism full-time, but he remained unyielding. His love of art was too strong—he wanted to be an outstanding artist.

For five years this battle raged in his breast. Finally he

39

came to the end of his will and surrendered fully and completely to the will of the Lord. He said, "It was then that a new day was ushered into my life. I became an evangelist and discovered that deep down in my soul was hidden a talent hitherto unknown to me. God had hidden a song in my heart, and touching a tender chord, He caused me to sing songs I had never sung before."

While in the home of George Sebring in East Palestine, Ohio and while reflecting on his most important decision, he wrote his famous "I Surrender All."

> **All to Jesus I surrender,**
> **All to Him I freely give;**
> **I will ever love and trust Him,**
> **In His presence daily live.**

Chorus:

> **I surrender all; I surrender all.**
> **All to Thee, my blessed Saviour,**
> **I surrender all.**

> **All to Jesus I surrender,**
> **Humbly at His feet I bow;**
> **Worldly pleasures all forsaken,**
> **Take me, Jesus, take me now.**

> **All to Jesus I surrender;**
> **Make me, Saviour, wholly Thine.**
> **Let me feel the Holy Spirit—**
> **Truly know that Thou art mine.**

Reflection: Nothing brings greater and more complete happiness into the heart of a Christian than the total surrender of oneself to the will of God.

God Reveals Himself

How Great Thou Art

Psalm 92

"O LORD, how great are thy works! and thy thoughts are very deep."—Vs. 5.

If you were asked, "What is your favorite gospel song of praise?" and you answered, "How Great Thou Art," you would be in agreement with millions of others around the world. It has been recorded by thousands of singers.

I have learned about it from extensive research and from a personal friend, Victor Nischick, who visited in the home of the English missionary who brought the song to the English-speaking world.

The life of this great hymn began in 1886 on an estate in southern Sweden, and it was known in several countries before it finally reached the shores of the United States. Carl Boberg, who later became a member of the Swedish parliament and a successful editor, walked across the beautiful grounds of the coastal estate and during his walk was caught in a thunderstorm. He was in awe as he watched the sky go from gray to black and then to a beautiful blue.

He later put his response to this display of nature in the form of a poem that he titled "O Store Gud" (O Great God)—a song of adoration and praise. It was later set to a Swedish folk tune. In 1907 Manfred von Glehn translated it into German, and five years later a Russian pastor, Rev. Ivan Prokhanoff, translated it into the Russian language.

Some years later, English missionary Stuart Hine first heard the song in Russia. He was born in 1899, in Hammersmith Grove, a small hamlet in England, and was dedicated to the Lord by his parents in a Salvation Army meeting. He was led to Christ by Madame Annie Ryall on February 22, 1914, and was baptized shortly thereafter. He was influenced greatly by the teachings of Charles H. Spurgeon.

In 1931 Hine and his young wife went as missionaries to the Carpathian area of Russia, then a part of Czechoslovakia. There they heard a very meaningful hymn that happened to be a Russian translation of Carl Boberg's Swedish song.

Hine found *himself* one day in a thunderstorm as he strolled through the Carpathian Mountains. While the lightning flashed and the thunder rolled through the mountain range, his mind went to the Russian hymn that he had heard and that had become so dear to him. English verses began to form in his mind, verses that were suggested by portions of the Russian translation. He wrote a second verse some time later as he roamed through the forests of Romania with some of the young people of that region. A third verse was written before returning to England.

Stuart Hine and David Griffiths visited a camp in Sussex, England, in 1948 where displaced Russians were being held. Only two in the whole camp were Christians who would profess their belief. The testimony of one of them and his anticipation of the second coming of Christ inspired Hine to write the fourth stanza of his English version of the hymn.

Hine wrote a book, *Not You, but God,* which presents two additional, optional verses that he copyrighted in 1953 as a translation of the Russian version. Dr. J. Edwin Orr introduced Hine's "How Great Thou Art!" in the United States in 1954. Three years later, it began its orbit around the world and has touched the lives of millions since then.

In my possession is a prized copy of "How Great Thou Art!" in the Russian language. All four of the men who helped bring us this song—Boberg the Swede, Von Glehn the German, Prokhanoff the Russian and Hine the Englishman—carefully preserved its awesome message.

I personally held a letter in my hand from Hine's daughter, Sonia, dated March 16, 1989, which contained the somber news that Stuart Hine had died peacefully in his sleep two days before. His memorial service was held at the Gospel Hall on Martello Road, Walton-on-Naze, Essex, England, on March 23. Thus in quiet dignity ended the life on earth of a man whose long years had been dedicated to serving the Lord.

Reflection: God's majestic creations all testify to His omnipotence and His omniscience. As we look around us on the things He has made, we too stand in awe of the Creator, the Power of all the universe. And just think, this great God has chosen to live in my heart and yours and in all who have accepted His gift of love.

Gratitude

Come, Ye Thankful People, Come

Ephesians 5:1–21

"Giving thanks always for all things unto God and the Father in the name of our Lord Jesus Christ."—Vs. 20.

"I do this day, in the presence of God and my own soul, renew my covenant with God and solemnly determine henceforth to become His and to do His work as far as in me lies."

These astounding words of determination came from a sixteen-year-old lad in England in 1826.

Henry Alford came from a long line of clergymen. His father, grandfather and great-grandfather were all ministers of the Church of England before him. He too became an Anglican vicar.

Henry Alford was born in London in 1810 and was reared in that great city. After graduating from Trinity College, Cambridge, his first charge was in Wymeswold, Leicestershire. His gentle disposition, cheerful attitude and sheer genius catapulted him to fame and high honor. He reached the "top" in 1857 when he became the dean of Canterbury Cathedral.

He was a versatile man: an artist, organist, singer, composer of verse and superb preacher. His literary ability was climaxed with the completion of the *Greek Testament,* a commentary of four volumes, which required twenty years of hard labor.

It is reported that he loved to mingle with the common man. He never seemed to lose his vision of the pit from which he too had been lifted. He was thankful.

In the fall of 1844 while he was at Wymeswold, the people of this hamlet decided to have a harvest festival, rejoicing in the abundant harvest already gathered into their barns. For this particular occasion, Mr. Alford wrote a song which has been used since at Thanksgiving time, "Come, Ye Thankful People, Come." The first of four stanzas says:

> **Come, ye thankful people, come;**
> **Raise the song of harvest-home.**
> **All is safely gathered in**
> **Ere the winter storms begin;**
> **God, our Maker, doth provide**
> **For our wants to be supplied.**
> **Come to God's own temple, come;**
> **Raise the song of harvest-home.**

Reflection: After you learn and sing this inspiring song, won't you rededicate yourself to a life of thankfulness? Learn to see and appreciate the little things that you so often overlook. Talk to God for a while. Thank Him and refrain from asking anything for yourself.

A Great Source of Inspiration

In the Garden

John 20:1–18

"Jesus saith unto her, Mary. She turned herself, and saith unto him, Rabboni; which is to say, Master."—Vs. 16.

"He looked a little like a Southern colonel with his white mustache, and he always appeared at the office with a small flower in his lapel. His marvelous sense of humor and dry wit could be very caustic if he thought the occasion demanded it—a truly brilliant man...."

This is a description of the late C. Austin Miles, given to me by Mrs. H. A. Dye, a friend of Mr. Miles.

His hymn "In the Garden" has, according to various polls, become the second-most-popular gospel song in the United States, with more than a million recordings having been sold.

One day in March 1912, Mr. Miles was studying the twentieth chapter of John, which records the story of Mary's coming to the garden to visit the tomb of Jesus. As she looked in, her heart sank because He wasn't there. Then when He spoke to her, she recognized Him, and her heart jumped for joy. She cried, "Rabboni"!

Mr. Miles imagined that he was present with them in the garden on that glorious occasion. He leaped from his chair, inspired to write the verses of this great song. Later that same evening he wrote the music that has accompanied it on its worldwide circulation.

Mr. Miles often remarked in his later years that he would make it through another year if he could get through the month of March. Oddly enough, he passed away on March 10, 1946, in Pitman, New Jersey.

The first verse of his song says:

I come to the garden alone,

> **While the dew is still on the roses,**
> **And the voice I hear,**
> **Falling on my ear,**
> **The Son of God discloses.**

Chorus:

> **And He walks with me, and He talks with me,**
> **And He tells me I am His own;**
> **And the joy we share as we tarry there,**
> **None other has ever known.**

Reflection: Our joy is made perfect as we share that joy with others—the joy of knowing in a personal way the Saviour spoken of in the Scripture reading for this article. When one seeks his own happiness, he loses real and satisfying happiness. But when he turns aside to notice the plight of others and gives help, the joy of the Saviour overtakes him.

Harpooned by His Own Crew

Amazing Graze

Ephesians 2:1–18

"For by grace are ye saved through faith; and that not of yourselves: it is the gift of God: Not of works, lest any man should boast."—Vss. 8, 9.

On the high seas in the mid 1700s, an angry sailor threw a whaling harpoon at his own captain, who had fallen overboard. What on earth would have provoked such anger and mutinous behavior?

The captain, John Newton, was a wicked, loathsome and cruel taskmaster, with little regard for his crew or the human cargo chained in the hold of his slave ship. The harpoon caught Newton in his hip, and he was hauled back on board, much like a large fish. The injury caused him to limp for the rest of his life.

Newton, born in London, England, in 1725, had been going to sea since age ten, after only three years of formal schooling. His first voyage was to the Mediterranean region with his father, captain of the ship. This seemed to be the only way the older Newton knew how to care for his young son, whose mother had died shortly before his seventh birthday.

Until his mother's death, he had learned Scripture passages, poems and hymns at her knee. Most of her time, he later revealed, was spent with his care and education. By his own testimony, at age four he could readily read "in any common book."

His early background and training were soon repressed as he associated with older, hardened sailors aboard his father's ship. As a result, he grew to be more wretched than almost anyone with whom he associated. His lifestyle led to rebellion, desertion, public floggings, abuse, destitution and near drowning.

48

Once while in the employ of a slave trader, he became ill and was left on the coast of Africa in the charge of a woman who locked him away and very nearly starved him to death. Only the kindness of the slaves in chains kept him alive, as they shared with him morsels of their meager allotment of food.

Often while enduring these horrid experiences, he thought back to his mother's instructions and guidance, striving to bring himself to a more religious state, but to no avail. He would read from the Bible, especially on Sundays. Afterward, he would lapse into an even more wicked state and try to influence others to join him in his sinful disregard for things holy and decent. While in this condition, Newton seemed to be totally unaware of God's marvelous grace in sparing his life time and again.

He was made the captain of his own ship at a very early age. After a particularly harrowing experience during a violent storm at sea when he despaired of his own life, Newton began to seek earnestly a right relationship with God. He had been reading *Imitation of Christ* by Thomas á Kempis. Apparently the book had a profound influence on his thinking.

Sometime later, on a small island off the coast of north Africa, sick and alone, he experienced the amazing grace about which he would later so eloquently write.

The following is part of his written account:

> Weak and delirious, I arose from my bed and crept to a secluded part of the island; there I found a renewed liberty to pray. I made no more resolves but cast myself before the Lord to do with me as He should please. I was enabled to hope and believe in a crucified Saviour. The burden was removed from my conscience.

He, at that time and by God's grace, began a new life. He married his sweetheart of many years and began to study for the ministry, later becoming the pastor of a small church in Olney, England. While there, he wrote many hymns and sacred songs. In 1779 he published a collection entitled the *Olney Hymns,* one of which was "Amazing Grace." The captivating melody to which the lyrics are sung was written some fifty years later. Here are three of its stanzas:

> **Amazing grace! how sweet the sound**
> **That saved a wretch like me!**
> **I once was lost, but now am found;**
> **Was blind, but now I see.**
>
> **'Twas grace that taught my heart to fear,**
> **And grace my fears relieved;**
> **How precious did that grace appear**
> **The hour I first believed!**
>
> **Through many dangers, toils and snares,**
> **I have already come;**
> **'Tis grace that brought me safe thus far,**
> **And grace will lead me Home.**

Remember the harpooning incident? Well, Newton later said, "Each limp is a constant reminder of God's grace to this wretched sinner."

He passed away at age eighty-two. Following are the first few lines of his epitaph, written by his own hand and, according to his instructions, inscribed on a simple slab of marble and mounted near his burial place:

> John Newton, clerk, once an infidel and libertine, a servant of slaves in Africa, was by the rich mercy of our Lord and Saviour, Jesus Christ, restored, pardoned and appointed to preach the Gospel which he had long labored to destroy.

Reflection: The miracle of amazing grace was experienced in a profound, dramatic fashion by the famous hymn writer himself. You too can experience that grace!

He Wouldn't Do It for Money

What a Friend We Have in Jesus

Romans 15:1–7

"We then that are strong ought to bear the infirmities of the weak, and not to please ourselves."—Vs. 1.

The town is Port Hope, Canada. A monument is being erected, not for the leading citizen who just died, but for a poor, unselfish workingman who gave most of his life and energy to help those who couldn't repay him.

Joseph Scriven was born in Dublin, Ireland, in 1819. He entered Trinity College in Dublin but after a short time left and joined the army. His health was not good enough for him to be an active soldier, so his military career was cut short, and he reentered college and earned his degree.

In his youth, Scriven had the prospect of becoming a great citizen with high ideals and great aspirations. He was engaged to a lovely lass who had promised to share his exalted dreams; however, on the eve of their wedding, her body was pulled from a pond into which she had fallen and drowned.

Young Scriven never overcame the shock. Although a college graduate and ready to embark on a brilliant career, he began to wander to try to forget his sorrow. At the age of twenty-five his travels took him to Port Hope, Canada, where he spent the last forty-one of his sixty-six years.

He fell in love again and planned to marry a wonderful young Canadian woman. Again, tragedy came his way, and she died after contracting pneumonia.

He became a very devout Christian. His beliefs, as a member of the Plymouth Brethren Church, led him to do servile labor for poor widows and the sick. He often served for no wages and was regarded by the people of the community as a kind man, but one who was an eccentric.

51

It was not known that Scriven had any poetic gifts until a short time before his death. A friend, sitting with him in an illness, discovered a poem that he had written to his mother in a time of sorrow, not intending that anyone else should see it. He had titled it "Pray Without Ceasing." He had not been able, financially, to go to see his mother; but he thought the poem would, perhaps, bring some comfort to her in her time of need.

When the friend inquired of Scriven who had written the poem, he replied, "The Lord and I did it between us."

The friend who discovered Scriven's verses was responsible for having them published in a book of poems, *Hymns and Other Verses*. The first verse reads:

> **What a Friend we have in Jesus,**
>   **All our sins and griefs to bear!**
> **What a privilege to carry**
>   **Ev'rything to God in prayer!**
> **Oh, what peace we often forfeit,**
>   **Oh, what needless pain we bear,**
> **All because we do not carry**
>   **Ev'rything to God in prayer!**

The poem was later set to music by a talented musician of the day, Charles Converse, and titled "What a Friend We Have in Jesus." It is said to be one of the first songs that many missionaries teach their converts. In the polls taken to determine the popularity of hymns and gospel songs, "What a Friend We Have in Jesus" is always near the top.

One morning in 1886, Scriven's body was pulled from Rice Lake in Ontario. It was not known exactly why he died in the water. Scriven will long be remembered as the one who helped others when they couldn't help themselves.

If you have read the other devotionals in this book, you have seen that the overriding attitude of philosophy in Christianity can be wrapped up in one word: others. We come back to it over and over again. Anything done for

Christ must be done for others.

Reflection: Prayer, as presented in this song, is the most powerful force available to Christians. Any person who neglects the opportunity to commune with God and draw on His resources will not show much growth in his faith. So will you now reaffirm your commitment to pray more?

A Hit From the Start

Battle Hymn of the Republic

Luke 21:20–33
*"And then shall they see the Son of man coming in a cloud with power and great glory."—*Vs. 27.

Very seldom do people of the world pick a sacred song, done in a simple yet beautiful way, and make a "hit" of it. But such was the case with Julia Ward Howe's "Battle Hymn of the Republic."

This song, born out of the Civil War and set to the tune of "John Brown's Body," is a great contribution by a very talented woman.

During the Civil War the soldiers used the song "John Brown's Body" as a marching tune. It has a snappy rhythm. Hearing this tune many times, Mrs. Howe often prayed that she might write more suitable words for such a melody.

With her husband and some friends, one day she rode just outside Washington to watch the reviewing of some army troops. During the course of the day she heard the soldiers singing the song. One of her companions turned and asked her why she didn't write some good words to that tune.

In recounting the story of her song, she said that she awakened the next morning before dawn thinking of the tune and framing verses in her mind. She later said, "I sprang out of bed and in the dimness found an old stump of a pen and scrawled the verses almost without looking at the paper."

Her lyrics, sung to the marching tune, were received with much enthusiasm and published in the *Atlantic Monthly* in February 1862. The song became very dear to Abraham Lincoln and was widely used during his presidency.

In 1965, it was used at the funeral services of Sir Winston Churchill. In more recent times it was often heard in activities surrounding the tragedies of September 11, 2001, in

54

New York, Washington and Pennsylvania.

Julia Howe lived nearly a century and did some wonderful things for which she is still remembered, but she is most famous for writing "Battle Hymn of the Republic."

Surely, you can sing this!

> **Mine eyes have seen the glory**
> **Of the coming of the Lord;**
> **He is trampling out the vintage**
> **Where the grapes of wrath are stored;**
> **He hath loosed the fateful lightning**
> **Of His terrible swift sword;**
> **His truth is marching on.**

Chorus:

> **Glory! glory, hallelujah!**
> **Glory! glory, hallelujah!**
> **Glory! glory, hallelujah!**
> **His truth is marching on.**

Now verse four:

> **In the beauty of the lilies**
> **Christ was born across the sea,**
> **With a glory in His bosom**
> **That transfigures you and me;**
> **As He died to make men holy,**
> **Let us die to make men free,**
> **While God is marching on.**

Reflection: The great God whom we serve, magnified in this song, is not only a God of terrible wrath against those who disobey Him, but a God of divine justice and unending truth. Great men—as the world counts greatness—live and die and are acclaimed for a while. But God continues to march on. How wonderful to know that He sees us, knows all about us and cares for us!

An Immigrant's Greatest Song

God Bless America

Psalm 33

"Let thy mercy, O LORD, be upon us, according as we hope in thee."—Vs. 22.

From large athletic stadiums filled with thousands of fans, to the steps of the Capitol Building where U.S. senators had gathered, to massive cathedrals with majestic spires, packed with reflective audiences, millions around the world watched by television as they all sang what has become our nation's prayer and our rallying cry, "God Bless America."

Kate Smith first sang this Irving Berlin composition on Armistice Day in 1939, launching it on its flight across the United States and into our hearts.

Irving Berlin was born Israel Baline in Eastern Russia on May 11, 1888. Young Israel was exposed to music early in life: his father, Moses Baline, was a cantor in the synagogue. The family moved to New York in 1893 to escape the pogroms in Russia.

As a young man, Irving became a singing waiter in a Chinatown cafe in New York City. By 1907 he had published his first song and, in 1911, wrote his first big, international hit, "Alexander's Ragtime Band."

Over the next fifty years he wrote hundreds of songs, many of which swept across America—songs such as "White Christmas" and "Always." But all of these pale into insignificance when we consider his song of thanksgiving and homage to his beloved country, "God Bless America."

Particularly since the events of September 11, 2001, in every corner and on countless occasions we hear it.

This "solemn prayer" for America has already been answered in countless ways and in millions of lives. We are so blessed to live, laugh and love in freedom—freedom to enjoy all that our hearts hold dear.

Along with Berlin, we recognize that God has singularly blessed our nation, from the peaceful Atlantic that bathes our eastern shores to the restless Pacific in the West, from the massive Great Lakes in the north to the winding Rio Grande that borders us to the south. The unique cities and towns that dot our land, the rolling hills, the spacious plains, the majestic mountains, the colorful deserts—all make up what we lovingly call America. We are so blessed, and truly this is our "home sweet home."

We are a diverse population, gathered from the four corners of the earth, working together to make America a unique and unparalleled nation in which to live, move and have our being.

Approaching our country through New York Harbor and passing by "Lady Liberty"—erected just seven years before Irving Berlin's family arrived—one can see the message she displays: "...Give me your tired, your poor, Your huddled masses yearning to breathe free....Send these, the homeless, tempest-tost to me...."

America offers to share her blessings with people of every hue, nationality and ethnic origin and invites all to live in this great land of opportunity.

The next time you hear or have the opportunity to join in the singing of "God Bless America," let its message mean as much to you as it apparently did to its composer. He donated millions of dollars in royalties to organizations such as God Bless America Fund, Army Emergency Relief and Boy Scouts and Girl Scouts of America.

He received the Congressional gold medal for "God Bless America" and other patriotic songs from President Eisenhower in 1955, and the Presidential Medal of Freedom from President Ford in 1977. Berlin loved his country.

He died in his sleep at his home in New York City on September 22, 1989, at age 101.

Reflection: Since September 11, 2001, this has become the nation's song and prayer. Make it your daily prayer that the Lord will truly bless our nation with guidance from above and love for our fellow Americans. Let us pray for America and her leaders every day.

It Almost Went Into the Fire

I Gave My Life for Thee

I Timothy 2:1–6
"For there is one God, and one mediator between God and men, the man Christ Jesus; Who gave himself a ransom for all, to be testified in due time."—Vss. 5,6.

Wherever the Christian message has gone in the world, women have been lifted from bondage and suppression and placed in a higher position. Some of the greatest contributions to mankind have been made by the fairer sex.

Elizabeth Barrett Browning had this to say about the women around Christ at the time of the crucifixion:

> **Not she with traitorous kiss her Saviour stung;**
> **Not she denied Him with unholy tongue;**
> **She, while apostles shrank, could danger brave,**
> **Last at His cross, and earliest at His grave.**

Frances Ridley Havergal, a British songwriter, is one of those whose contributions to the spreading of the Christian message is deemed very great indeed! Though her body was sickly, her life radiated with the love of her Saviour.

Being brought up in the home of a preacher of the Gospel contributed greatly to her fine character. She launched her poetic ventures at age seven and later began the study of music, becoming an accomplished singer and pianist.

Fifteen years after the writing of "I Gave My Life for Thee," Miss Havergal related that the song very nearly went into the fire instead of around the world. She said that it was the very first thing she wrote that could be called a hymn, written in 1858, when she was only twenty-one.

She did not, it seems, realize what she was writing about. She felt that she was following Christ very far off, always doubting and fearing. Her faith seemed weak, not the real faith that Christ wants His followers to have. Scribbling the

59

words of the hymn on the back of a circular, she read them over; then deciding it was not even poetry, she chose not to write it out completely.

As she was reaching out her hand to put it in the fire, a sudden impulse caused her to draw it back. She crumpled it and put it in her pocket.

A few days later as she visited an old friend in the almshouse, the poor lady began talking about her love for the Saviour. Miss Havergal thought of the poem she had written, pulled the verses out of her pocket and began to read them to her. The lady was very delighted with the poem, causing Miss Havergal to take further pains to write the verses out. From that point, they have gone from country to country, blessing the hearts of millions.

A finer song of consecration cannot be found anywhere. Her father, William Havergal, wrote the melody to which the poem was first sung. P. P. Bliss, an American songwriter and singer who wrote "Hold the Fort" and "Let the Lower Lights Be Burning," later wrote the melody that we hear today. His melody has become much more popular in America.

There are four stanzas to this lovely song. Here is the first one:

> **I gave My life for thee;**
> **My precious blood I shed,**
> **That thou might'st ransomed be**
> **And quickened from the dead.**
> **I gave, I gave My life for thee;**
> **What hast thou giv'n for Me?**

Frances Havergal also wrote the very popular "Take My Life, and Let It Be" and my favorite, "Like a River Glorious."

Reflection: "I Gave My Life for Thee" is a beautiful reminder of the Scriptures that describe what Christ has done for each of us. The question, "What hast thou giv'n for Me?" should bring conviction to all of us.

Little Things Are Important

I Need Thee Every Hour

Hebrews 13:1–6
"Let your conversation be without covetousness; and be content with such things as ye have: for he hath said, I will never leave thee, nor forsake thee."—Vs. 5.

The famous pastor and hymn writer, Robert Lowry, joined hands and hearts with one of his parishioners, Annie Sherwood Hawks, to give America and the world one of the great hymns of comfort and devotion.

Annie Sherwood Hawks was born in Hoosick, New York on May 28, 1836. Very early on, she developed a love for poetry, even writing some while still in grade school. Her first poem was published when she was fourteen. She married Charles Hawks, and they were blessed with three children.

One morning in her home, Annie was happily busy about the chores at hand. She gives testimony that her home seemed to take on the light of Heaven, and she seemed to be in the very presence of God. As the words, "I need Thee every hour," flashed into her mind, she hurriedly found pencil and paper and began to write. Phrases flowed from her pencil. In just a few moments she had completed a poem, "I Need Thee Every Hour," the first stanza of which is:

> **I need Thee ev'ry hour,**
> **Most gracious Lord;**
> **No tender voice like Thine**
> **Can peace afford.**

The tune and chorus were written by Dr. Lowry. These additions have done more than a little to carry the song to a wide audience.

It was first sung at the National Baptist Sunday School Convention in Cincinnati, Ohio in 1872. From there it made its way into a hymnal published by Lowry and William H.

Doane, titled the *Royal Diadem*. Ira Sankey made it more popular when he used it in the Moody-Sankey meetings. The song has been translated into several other languages.

Mrs. Hawks personally experienced the comforting power of her song only a few years later when her husband went to be with the Lord. She joined him in Heaven in 1918.

Your life will become more dedicated when you realize that Christ is interested in every aspect of your being. He takes notice of the minutest detail of your existence. Everyday tasks, like those of Mrs. Hawks, are hallowed by His concern and presence.

Sing the second verse and chorus thoughtfully:

> **I need Thee ev'ry hour;**
> **Stay Thou nearby;**
> **Temptations lose their pow'r**
> **When Thou art nigh.**

Chorus:

> **I need Thee, oh, I need Thee;**
> **Ev'ry hour I need Thee!**
> **Oh, bless me now, my Saviour,**
> **I come to Thee!**

Reflection: God sees you—NOW! He knows all about you—NOW! And He cares for you—NOW!

Longing for Something to Sing

When the Roll Is Called Up Yonder

I Corinthians 15:51–58

"In a moment, in the twinkling of an eye, at the last trump: for the trumpet shall sound, and the dead shall be raised incorruptible, and we shall be changed."—Vs. 52.

James M. Black was a Sunday school teacher and president of the young people's society in a church in Canada. He was quite young at the time. One day he met a girl, fourteen years of age, poorly clothed and the child of a drunkard. It was evident that she did not enjoy the nicer things of life that many teenagers enjoyed. Young Black was moved to invite her to attend Sunday school and to join the young people's group, thinking this would be a great blessing and help to her and might even win her to Christ.

One evening at a consecration meeting, when each member answered the roll call by repeating a Scripture text, the girl failed to respond. This situation brought the thought to Black's mind that it would be a very sad thing if our names are called from the Lamb's book of life in Heaven and we should be absent. The thought, although not theologically sound, brought this prayer to his lips: "O God, when my name is called up yonder, may I be there to respond!"

He then longed for something suitable to sing but found nothing in the books at hand. He closed the meeting that night and, while on his way home, was still wishing that there might be a song that could be sung on such an occasion. All of a sudden the thought came: *Why don't you write such a song?* He tried to dismiss the idea, thinking that he could never accomplish that.

When Black reached his house, his wife saw that he was deeply troubled and questioned him about his problem, but he did not reply. He only thought of the song that he would like to write. All of a sudden, like a dayspring, the first stanza came in full. He later said that in fifteen minutes he had composed the other two verses. He then went to the piano and played the music just as you will find it in the hymnals today—note for note. It has never been changed.

Verse one reads:

When the trumpet of the Lord shall sound and
time shall be no more
And the morning breaks, eternal, bright and
fair;
When the saved of earth shall gather over on the
other shore
And the roll is called up yonder, I'll be there.

Chorus:

When the roll is called up yonder,
When the roll is called up yonder,
When the roll is called up yonder,
When the roll is called up yonder, I'll be there.

As told in a later chapter, James Black faced tragedy in his life, including being kidnapped at age eight. Some years later, while on a ship, he learned that his house had burned. God used it all to make him a blessing to those around him and, through his songs, to us as well.

Reflection: God can preserve the life of a kidnapped lad, bring him into circumstances that would lead him to a saving knowledge of Christ and make him a blessing by causing him to write a song that rings around the world in many languages. Surrendered, you can be of great service to God also—perhaps not in that way, but in His way and time and according to the gifts He has given to you.

A Mom's Suggestion

I'd Rather Have Jesus

Mark 8:34–38
"For what shall it profit a man, if he shall gain the whole world, and lose his own soul?"—Vs. 36.

"America's beloved gospel singer" is a title given to George Beverly Shea that no other contemporary Christian singer has ever approached. His rich bass voice, coupled with his sincere Christian attitude, have carried him to the zenith of man's acclaim for gospel soloists.

On February 5, 1961, Mr. Shea was the soloist at a one-day mammoth rally at one of the athletic stadiums in Tampa, Florida. Afterward it was my privilege to interview him concerning his song "I'd Rather Have Jesus." The following is the sum and substance of what he told me:

"I wrote 'I'd Rather Have Jesus' in 1933. As I sat one evening playing the piano, my mother brought to me a piece of paper on which was written a poem by Rhea Miller. She thought it to be a very wonderful poem and wanted me to read it. 'Will you try your hand at writing a melody for it?' she asked. I began to play as a melody came to me. The melody seemed to fit the lyric, and so I began to sing and play for the first time 'I'd Rather Have Jesus.'"

Mr. Shea was born in Winchester, Ontario, Canada. He had the advantage of good musical training early in life. He was educated at Houghton College. In earlier years Shea had his share of the lucrative offers of this world, but he thoughtfully turned them down to become a singing servant for the Saviour.

When the rich voice of George Beverly Shea is but a memory, many happy Christians will still be singing "I'd Rather Have Jesus."

Reflection: According to the teachings of Christ, this is one of the most difficult songs to sing and really mean it. When we gain the victory over our desire for more and more of what this world has to offer, we have come much closer to real fellowship with the Saviour.

Music From the Attic

Joy to the World!

Matthew 1:18–2:12

"When they saw the star, they rejoiced with exceeding great joy."—2:10.

Three men from three countries, whose lives and works spanned nearly two centuries, each played a major role in bringing to us one of our most joyous and beloved carols.

The story begins in Germany in 1692. It was a very quiet night in the Handel household. All were sleeping—at least Mr. and Mrs. Handel thought so. Suddenly awakened to the sound of music in the middle of the night, they sat up in the bed wondering, *Where is that music coming from?*

Searching through the house, they could not find it. Still they could hear music. Suddenly they said, "The attic!" Their seven-year-old son, George, slept up there. When they opened his door, they were astonished to see him sitting in his room playing a small pianolike instrument called a clavier.

Not only were the Handels unaware that their son could play music, they didn't know that his uncle had secretly helped George move an instrument to his attic room!

Young Handel became a prominent musician, writing many popular songs and musicals. He traveled to England where his music found favor with royalty and noblemen, which led to fame and fortune.

At age fifty-six, he began to reflect on his accomplishments. His music had been adored by thousands, he had performed his compositions before kings and queens, but he was not satisfied. He wanted to write something much greater, something that would bring joy to humanity and make people better.

The teachings of his devout Christian mother had a profound influence on his life and values. After a season of earnest prayer, asking God to help him compose something of importance, he began to write. For almost three weeks he labored day and night, taking only short breaks for a bit of rest and nourishment.

He came from this ordeal a victor. He had written his immortal *Messiah,* an oratorio that has since been sung more than any other ever penned. In 1999, *USA Today* reported that an estimated 125,000 people in the United States would listen to the *Messiah* during the Christmas season.

Now for the rest of the story.

During the years Handel was composing, in another part of England lived Isaac Watts, a man only about five feet tall but a literary giant—a theologian and a poet. He had begun writing verses as a small child. Once his father scolded him because he made up rhymes as he talked to people. After the scolding, Isaac replied, "O Father, do some pity take, and I will no more verses make."

When Isaac was a teenager and complained that the songs sung in church were hard to sing, his father said, "Well, write some that are better."

And so he did. For the next two years he wrote a new hymn every week. English critics have concluded that his "When I Survey the Wondrous Cross" is the greatest hymn in the English language.

The people of England loved another of his poems as well. It is based on Psalm 98, and it brought "joy" to the hearts of all who read it.

Now our story moves to America.

Nearly a century later a Boston composer and music publisher, Lowell Mason, found Watts's poem of "joy" and wanted very much to publish it. There was only one problem—he didn't have a proper musical setting.

In his search, he came upon a beautiful melody in Handel's music. And so Lowell Mason published Isaac Watts's poem, set to George Handel's tune, thus creating one of the world's most beloved and popular Christmas carols, "Joy to the World."

This is the first of four stanzas:

> **Joy to the world! the Lord is come;**
> **Let earth receive her King.**
> **Let ev'ry heart prepare Him room,**
> **And Heav'n and nature sing.**

Reflection: In every corner of the globe where men have carried the message of Christ, it has brought joy. Christ sets the captive free and puts a song in their hearts. The King reigns in the hearts of men to bring joy when they hear the message, "Joy to the world! the Lord is come."

My Sunbeam

The Ninety and Nine

Matthew 18:1–14

"Even so it is not the will of your Father which is in heaven, that one of these little ones should perish."—Vs. 14.

Among the poor and suffering, Elizabeth Clephane was known as "My Sunbeam." She was born in Edinburgh in 1830. At an early age she learned the meaning of sorrow through the loss of her parents. This very bright child had a vivid imagination and a passionate love for poetry. She was first in her class and was, as reported, a favorite pupil.

As she grew older, she gave all of her money, beyond the bare necessities, to charities.

For a friend, she wrote a poem which found its way to a newspaper. Ira Sankey purchased a copy of the paper as he was traveling with D. L. Moody through Scotland on their way to Edinburgh for three days of meetings.

As Mr. Sankey rode along, he read the newspaper, then cast it aside, to pick it up again just as the journey was ending. In one corner was a poem which he read with great interest. He clipped it and slipped it into his vest pocket, the seed-plot from which sprang many gospel songs that are now known throughout the world.

At the noon meeting on the second day, Mr. Moody presented a message entitled "The Good Shepherd." At the end, he called on Dr. Bonar to say a few words. When Dr. Bonar finished, Mr. Moody turned to Mr. Sankey and asked if he had an appropriate song for the close of the service. Frantically, he began to search for a song. Suddenly, thinking of the poem that he had stuffed in his vest pocket, Mr. Sankey stepped to the small organ, his hands fell on the keys, he struck an A-flat chord and, composing as he went, began to sing for the first time "The Ninety and Nine." The words and music remain unchanged.

A short time later, Mr. Sankey received a letter from Elizabeth Clephane's sister thanking him for singing the words written by Elizabeth, who had already gone to be with her Shepherd.

> **There were ninety and nine that safely lay**
>   **In the shelter of the fold,**
> **But one was out on the hills away,**
>   **Far off from the gates of gold—**
> **Away on the mountains wild and bare,**
> **Away from the tender Shepherd's care,**
> **Away from the tender Shepherd's care.**

Here is the fifth verse:

> **But all through the mountains, thunder riv'n,**
>   **And up from the rocky steep,**
> **There arose a glad cry to the gate of Heav'n,**
>   **"Rejoice! I have found My sheep!"**
> **And the angels echoed around the throne,**
> **"Rejoice, for the Lord brings back His own!**
> **Rejoice, for the Lord brings back His own."**

Reflection: Perhaps the most wonderful thing about the Christian religion is that we, as individuals, are important in the eyes of God.

The Night the Lights Went Out

Let the Lower Lights Be Burning

Matthew 5:1–17

"Let your light so shine before men, that they may see your good works, and glorify your Father which is in heaven."—Vs. 16.

Philip P. Bliss was one of the most prolific songwriters in America during the nineteenth century. Only the Lord knows what he might have done had he not died at age thirty-eight. He was sometimes called the golden-voiced Bliss.

Bliss was born on July 9, 1838, in Clearfield County, Pennsylvania. Since his family was poor, he began making his own living at age eleven. He had a passon for music and spent as much time in the pursuit of a music education as possible.

He became an accomplished musician and moved to Chicago where he established a profitable music business, which included the writing and publishing of secular songs.

He made a formal, complete surrender of his talents to the Lord at the urging of men such as D. L. Moody and Major D. W. Whittle. From that time forward, his golden voice and talented pen were mightily used of the Lord. We still sing his songs—"Jesus Loves Even Me," "Hold the Fort" and the musical setting for "It Is Well With My Soul," to name just a few.

Philip Bliss was in the congregation of Dwight L. Moody when he heard Moody tell this story:

> On a dark, stormy night, when the waves rolled like mountains and not a star was to be seen, a boat, rocking and plunging, neared the Cleveland harbor.
>
> "Are you sure this is Cleveland?" asked the captain, seeing only one light from the lighthouse.
>
> "Quite sure, sir," replied the pilot.

"Where are the lower lights?"

"Gone out, sir."

"Can you make the harbor?"

"We must, or perish, sir!"

With a strong hand and a brave heart, the old pilot turned the wheel. But, alas, in the darkness he missed the channel, and with a crash upon the rocks the boat was shivered, and many a life was lost in a watery grave.

Brethren, the Master will take care of the great lighthouse; let us keep the lower lights burning!

As P. P. Bliss sat there, his heart was touched deeply. His alert mind began to work rapidly, and at the very next service he sang a new song. The first of three stanzas goes like this:

> **Brightly beams our Father's mercy**
> **From His lighthouse evermore,**
> **But to us He gives the keeping**
> **Of the lights along the shore.**

Chorus:

> **Let the lower lights be burning!**
> **Send a gleam across the wave!**
> **Some poor fainting, struggling seaman**
> **You may rescue, you may save.**

God has allowed only a few to write these wonderful gospel songs, but He has allowed millions in many lands to sing songs like "Let the Lower Lights Be Burning."

Philip P. Bliss was the victim of a horrible train accident in 1876. He had gotten out safely, then, discovering that his wife was still in the burning train, he went back to try to bring her to safety. Both perished in the fire.

Reflection: Often our lights flicker, grow dim and go out without our even being aware of it. Others read our lives whether or not we choose for them to do so. We will give account as to how we lead people in this world.

Not Hindered by Her Handicap

Rescue the Perishing

Psalm 126

"He that goeth forth and weepeth, bearing precious seed, shall doubtless come again with rejoicing, bringing his sheaves with him."—Vs. 6.

Fanny Crosby was deeply interested in gospel work among the poor who were down-and-out. One evening in New York she addressed a large company in the slum area. Her heart was moved at the close of her address as she heard a young boy, eighteen years of age, come forward and say, "I promised my mother to meet her in Heaven, but the way I am now living, that will be impossible."

After he had prayed, he arose with a new light in his eyes and exclaimed, "Since I have now found God, I will be meeting my mother in Heaven!"

As the service continued, her poetic mind began to work, and before she retired that evening she had completed the verses to a "battle cry" for the great army of Christian soldiers. Think of the lost as you sing verse one of "Rescue the Perishing."

> **Rescue the perishing; care for the dying;**
> **Snatch them in pity from sin and the grave.**
> **Weep o'er the erring one; lift up the fallen;**
> **Tell them of Jesus the mighty to save.**

Chorus:

> **Rescue the perishing;**
> **Care for the dying.**
> **Jesus is merciful;**
> **Jesus will save.**

To this writer, the third verse is the greatest bit of poetry ever written:

Down in the human heart, crushed by the tempter,
    Feelings lie buried that grace can restore;
Touched by a loving heart, wakened by kindness,
    Chords that are broken will vibrate once more.

Moody-Sankey meetings helped to popularize many of Fanny Crosby's eight thousand hymns and gospel songs in this country and in England. Her motto was, "I think that life is not too long; therefore, I determine that many people read a song who would not read a sermon."

Frances Jane Crosby was born in Putnam County, New York on March 24, 1820. Her sight was destroyed at the age of six weeks because of the misapplication of a poultice on her eyes. Blessed with a marvelous disposition, she accepted her handicap with an unusual display of courage.

She was born again in 1851. Seven years later she married a blind musician, Alexander Van Alstyne. Her cheerfulness and courage, coupled with the simple, childlike trust in divine watch care, enabled her to write such heartwarming hymns as "Blessed Assurance," "Near the Cross" and "Safe in the Arms of Jesus."

Friday morning, February 12, 1915, just prior to her ninety-fifth birthday, Fanny Crosby realized to the fullest the words she had written and recited many times, "And I shall see Him face to face."

Reflection: Fanny Crosby is another example of one who would not sit around and feel sorry for herself. Even in her blindness, her thoughts were constantly of others. Like her, we can find peace when we turn aside to help someone else. All of our service to Christ must be done for others.

Of Infinite Worth

His Eye Is on the Sparrow

Matthew 10:28–42

"Are not two sparrows sold for a farthing? and one of them shall not fall on the ground without your Father."

"Fear ye not therefore, ye are of more value than many sparrows."—Vss. 29, 31.

"God will take care of you" was a wonderful lyric that came from the pen of Mrs. Civilla D. Martin, a Canadian, but it was by no means her most famous song.

After her education in the schools of Nova Scotia, she became a schoolteacher. Before long she had met and married Dr. Walter Martin, an evangelist and musician of sorts, and joined him in his itinerant work. Her poem "God Will Take Care of You" was written for her husband who set it to music. Although she had written poetry for a number of years, it was the success of this song that gave her some idea that God could use her poetic ability.

Early in the 1900s, Mrs. Martin, hearing of a dear friend who had been overtaken with a severe state of depression, became quite burdened for her. She left their home, located on the campus of a Bible school in Johnson City, New York, and made her way by train to see the lady who lived in Elmira, New York.

While there, Mrs. Martin told her friend of an incident which happened a short time earlier, when she experienced God's protecting hand during an illness, hoping the story would be an encouragement to the depressed soul.

After hearing the story, her friend said, "You know, I shouldn't worry, should I? We are promised in the Bible that God watches over the little sparrows." Mrs. Martin agreed, "He surely does." They then had a little time of rejoicing over God's wonderful watch care and protection.

76

The journey back home was made shorter for Mrs. Martin by the satisfying realization that she had helped her friend. When she arrived home, she sat down and penned the words to one of the most beautiful and famous of all the gospel songs, "His Eye Is on the Sparrow." Her husband tried his hand at writing a musical setting, but they were not at all satisfied with it and sent the poem to Mr. Charles H. Gabriel, a famous songwriter, and asked him to write some fitting music for it. He did so, and his melody has been the vehicle that carried Mrs. Martin's poem around the world. It was first sung in 1905 by Charles M. Alexander during the Torrey-Alexander revival in Royal Albert Hall in England.

So encouraging are the verses of this magnificent song, I am quoting them in their entirety:

> **Why should I feel discouraged,**
> **Why should the shadows come,**
> **Why should my heart be lonely**
> **And long for Heav'n and home,**
> **When Jesus is my portion?**
> **My constant Friend is He;**
> **His eye is on the sparrow,**
> **And I know He watches me.**

Chorus:

> **I sing because I'm happy;**
> **I sing because I'm free;**
> **For His eye is on the sparrow,**
> **And I know He watches me.**

> **"Let not your heart be troubled,"**
> **His tender word I hear,**
> **And resting on His goodness,**
> **I lose my doubts and fears.**
> **Tho' by the path He leadeth**
> **But one step I may see,**
> **His eye is on the sparrow,**
> **And I know He watches me.**

Whenever I am tempted,
   Whenever clouds arise,
When songs give place to sighing,
   When hope within me dies,
I draw the closer to Him;
   From care He sets me free.
His eye is on the sparrow,
   And I know He watches me.

Reflection: None of us would ever fret or worry over a single problem if we could gain a deep-seated assurance that our Heavenly Father cares more for us than for all of His other earthly creatures. He cares more for us than we are able to care for ourselves.

Only One Song

My Jesus, I Love Thee

Psalm 28

"The LORD is my strength and my shield; my heart trusted in him, and I am helped: therefore my heart greatly rejoiceth; and with my song will I praise him."—Vs. 7.

Occasionally, in the search for information concerning the story behind a particular hymn, impenetrable barriers are encountered. Such is the case with one of America's best-loved hymns, "My Jesus, I Love Thee." Not until recent years was the identity of the songwriter known.

One doesn't often reach the pinnacle of his achievement at such a tender age as sixteen, but that was the case with a youth named William Featherstone of Montreal, Canada. Shortly after his conversion in 1862, he wrote a beautiful Christian song, a copy of which he sent to his aunt in Los Angeles. She then sent it to England where it was published in the *London Hymnbook* in 1864. As far as anyone knows, it was the only song young Featherstone wrote.

By way of the *London Hymnbook,* it came to the attention of Dr. A. J. Gordon, a well-known preacher and pastor in New England, who provided the musical setting that has helped make the verses so famous. It is virtually impossible to pick up a hymnal and find it omitted.

Dr. Adoniram Judson Gordon was born in New Hampshire on April 19, 1836. He graduated from Brown University and Newton Theological Seminary. Later he was pastor of a church in Jamaica Plain, Massachusetts.

One day while searching for hymns to go into a new hymnal he was compiling, he ran across "My Jesus, I Love Thee." Thinking the tune unsuitable, he composed what he thought was a more appropriate one. Soon the song was being sung across America.

It was not until after Dr. Gordon published his hymnal

79

that he found out the identity of the young man who wrote the lyrics.

A more beautiful hymn of consecration cannot be found. The first of the four stanzas reads:

My Jesus, I love Thee; I know Thou art mine.
For Thee all the follies of sin I resign.
My gracious Redeemer, my Saviour art Thou;
If ever I loved Thee, my Jesus, 'tis now.

Reflection: What Christ wants from us is our love, our faithfulness, our devotion. He died that we might know Him; He made a way for us to fellowship with Him—now and in Glory.

An Orphan Boy and a Blind Organist

Angels From the Realms of Glory

Luke 2:1–15

"And suddenly there was with the angel a multitude of the heavenly host praising God, and saying, Glory to God in the highest, and on earth peace, good will toward men."— Vss. 13, 14.

Angels have always fascinated us. What do they look like? Do they really fly? How big are they?

The Bible tells us about angels and their many tasks performed for the Heavenly Father. The song in this story has to do with a special group of angels and their most important announcement two thousand years ago.

This story took place many years ago in the country of Scotland. A six-year-old boy, James Montgomery, was sent off to a boarding school. His missionary parents believed that the boarding school was best for him. They wanted him to have the education the school would give him, because they actually wanted him to be a preacher.

James's parents set sail for the West Indies to begin their mission work. But soon after they arrived in the new country, they became very ill and both died.

You can imagine the hurt, the fear and the loneliness young James must have felt. As far as we know, he had no other family to care for him. But, as all children, he had his guardian angel. In the next few years that angel would have his hands full.

Although James was only ten years of age and still quite puzzled and sad, he began to write poems. Since he was not doing well in school, the teachers wondered if his loneliness was keeping him from studying. At age twelve his grades had gotten no better; in fact, he was failing in his schoolwork.

He was taken out of the school at age fourteen and put to

81

work in a grocery store. He was not at all happy with his situation, so at age sixteen, he ran away to the big city of London where he continued to write poems. He walked the streets trying to sell his works to passersby.

Sometime later he went to Sheffield, England, where he got a job as a printer's helper in a newspaper office, a job that he liked very much. He had not been working at the newspaper office very long when the owner, who had gotten into trouble with the government, ran off to America.

Although he was still very young, the newspaper office was left for James to run. It was not easy for someone so young to publish a newspaper, but he worked very hard. He changed the name of the paper to *Iris* and made it a successful newspaper. The orphan boy became a good citizen, and the people of Sheffield loved and respected him.

The *Iris* was such a success that James became a very wealthy man. Now he finally had someone to publish his poems—himself!

On Christmas Eve, 1816, at age forty-five, Montgomery published in his newspaper a very special poem which he called "Nativity." It was about the angels and their announcement concerning the birth of Jesus, the newborn King!

During that time there was a blind organist in England named Henry Smart. Before he became blind, he had written hundreds of songs. After he became blind, he still wanted to write songs, so he asked his daughter to help him. She would write down the notes as he played the organ.

Years later, James Montgomery's beautiful poem, "Nativity," was set to one of Henry Smart's tunes. The title was then changed to "Angels From the Realms of Glory." This beautiful Christmas carol has become very famous and is sung in many countries at Christmastime.

And so, the young orphan boy's work lives on in this wonderful carol. Here is the first stanza:

Angels from the realms of Glory,
    Wing your flight o'er all the earth;
Ye who sang creation's story
    Now proclaim Messiah's birth:
Come and worship, come and worship,
Worship Christ, the newborn King.

Reflection: It seems that the secret of success is still the willingness to work hard. For the Christian, willingness to work hard in a manner that pleases the Lord is even better.

Out of Darkness, a Sunbeam

O Love That Wilt Not Let Me Go

Romans 8:26–39

"Nay, in all these things we are more than conquerors through him that loved us."—Vs. 37.

The story behind this hymn is remarkably similar to the story behind the gospel song, "No One Ever Cared for Me Like Jesus." Both were born out of dark sorrow.

Dr. George Matheson was another of the great preachers produced by Scotland. He was born there in 1842. While still in his teens, he entered the University of Glasgow. He was stricken with total blindness shortly after his entrance into school, but not even this could stop George Matheson.

Before his death, Dr. Matheson recorded his own account of his masterpiece, "O Love That Wilt Not Let Me Go," a hymn composed in the manse of Innelan on the evening of June 6, 1882.

He was alone in the manse. It was the day of his sister's marriage, and the rest of the family were staying overnight in Glasgow. Some event, known only to him, caused him the most severe mental suffering. It has been suggested that being in love with a young lady who jilted him may have been the cause of his extreme distress. Nevertheless, the hymn was a fruit of that suffering.

He reported that the hymn was the quickest bit of work he had ever done. It seemed to be dictated to him by some inward voice. The whole work was completed in five minutes, and it received no retouching or correction.

Matheson possessed an extreme command of the English language. The Lord seems to have given him unusual insight to the truths he presents in his poem.

Albert L. Peace, who lived from 1844 to 1912, wrote the

musical setting that has carried this message to millions in numerous countries.

I quote four verses of what I consider some of the greatest poetry ever written:

> O Love that wilt not let me go,
> I rest my weary soul in Thee;
> I give Thee back the life I owe,
> That in Thine ocean depths its flow
>   May richer, fuller be.
>
> O Light that followest all my way,
> I yield my flickering torch to Thee;
> My heart restores its borrowed ray,
> That in Thy sunshine's glow its day
>   May brighter, fairer be.
>
> O Joy that seeketh me through pain,
> I cannot close my heart to Thee;
> I trace the rainbow through the rain
> And feel the promise is not vain
>   That morn shall tearless be.
>
> O Cross that liftest up my head,
> I dare not ask to hide from Thee;
> I lay in dust life's glory dead,
> And from the ground there blossoms red
>   Life that shall endless be.

Reflection: It is only tremendous love that God has for His children that causes Him to draw a curtain over our future so we cannot see what lies ahead. Therefore, we must cling to Him for daily strength and guidance. Truly this makes our lives richer and fuller.

A Pioneer Leaves a Song

The Eastern Gate

Psalm 30

"For his anger endureth but a moment; in his favour is life: weeping may endure for a night, but joy cometh in the morning."—Vs. 5.

The small town of Kirksville, Missouri was the birthplace of the Reverend I. G. Martin, one of the great songwriters of years gone by. Martin was born on April 18, 1862, and became a Christian at a very early age. Sometime after his conversion, he began to drift away from his commitment to the Lord.

After receiving his college training, Martin began a career as a teacher. This vocation was short-lived, however, and young Martin turned his attention to the stage, where he performed as an actor and singer. This led him further away from his profession of Christ as Saviour.

As the years went by, one day he found himself in a revival service in Milwaukee, Wisconsin where services were led by a Methodist evangelist named Tillotsen. P. P. Bilhorn was the singer and song leader for those meetings. After hearing the preaching and singing of those revivalists, Martin rededicated his life to Christ and determined to serve the Lord again. He later entered the ministry as an evangelistic singer.

Martin soon began to preach as well as sing. His travels carried him to many places in our nation where he spoke and sang in churches and camp meetings. During these years of ministry, he began to write songs that seemingly flowed eloquently from his soul.

In the early years of the Church of the Nazarene, Martin was appointed by Dr. Bresee as superintendent of the Eastern District, which consisted of the territory east of the Rocky Mountains. For six years he served the First

Nazarene Church in Chicago and later moved to Malden, Massachusetts.

Martin lived for over a century. He passed away in August 1967. Haldor Lillenas, who knew him for a portion of the fifty or more years that he preached the Gospel, said, "He was indeed one of the staunch pioneers of our church. He lived long and well, loved his Lord fervently, served his church faithfully and was a devoted husband and father."

Millions of Christians are glad that before he departed this life, I. G. Martin wrote a beautiful song about Heaven. And so, happily we sing "The Eastern Gate."

> **I will meet you in the morning,**
> **Just inside the Eastern Gate;**
> **Then be ready, faithful pilgrim,**
> **Lest with you it be too late.**

Chorus:

> **I will meet you in the morning,**
> **Just inside the Eastern Gate over there.**
> **I will meet you in the morning,**
> **I will meet you in the morning over there.**

> **Oh, the joy of that glad meeting**
> **With the saints who for us wait!**
> **What a blessed, happy meeting,**
> **Just inside the Eastern Gate.**

This wonderful song has experienced a revival of popularity in recent years. It is truly a favorite of thousands of Christians.

Reflection: When our loved ones are taken into the arms of God Himself, joy and peace unspeakable should flood our very souls as we anticipate the reunion in Heaven.

The Power of Song

A Mighty Fortress Is Our God

Hebrews 11:1–16

"But without faith it is impossible to please him: for he that cometh to God must believe that he is, and that he is a rewarder of them that diligently seek him."—Vs. 6.

It was on a cold, windy night that a man named Conrad heard a lad singing as he walked by his house. Conrad invited him in, gave him something to eat and let him warm himself.

Arrangements were made for the boy, Martin Luther, to live with Conrad and his family. They loved him, cared for him and sent him to school. He graduated with a doctor of philosophy degree.

He entered the Catholic priesthood and tried to serve well, but he could never find peace of heart and soul. He thought, *If only I could make the pilgrimage to Rome, these fears would vanish.*

He did make that pilgrimage. While crawling up the Holy Stairs on his knees (said to be the staircase moved from Pilate's judgment hall to Rome), he remembered the verse, "The just shall live by faith." So he sprang to his feet, and the Reformation began!

Later, to the amazement of everyone, Martin Luther started writing hymns and gospel songs. The people loved them so dearly that the Catholic ecclesiastics said that the songs of Martin Luther were destroying more souls than all his writings and sermons.

He preached long and hard and became a forceful leader of one of the world's greatest revivals.

On his tomb is inscribed A MIGHTY FORTRESS IS OUR GOD, the name of his famous hymn, said to be "the greatest hymn of the greatest man in the greatest period in German history."

It is a paraphrase of Psalm 46. The first stanza reads:

A mighty Fortress is our God,
A Bulwark never failing;
Our helper He amid the flood
Of mortal ills prevailing.
For still our ancient foe
Doth seek to work us woe;
His craft and pow'r are great,
And, armed with cruel hate,
On earth is not his equal.

There are three additional powerful stanzas.

Frederick H. Hedge translated it from the German in 1853. Christians have been singing it for over four hundred years, and it is still a soul-stirring hymn.

Reflection: To have faith in God is a Christian's greatest asset. Faith enables one to do his best for God at all times. It is really an evidence of our true love for Him.

A Prayer That Became a Song

Rock of Ages

I Corinthians 10:1–13

"And did all drink the same spiritual drink: for they drank of that spiritual Rock that followed them: and that Rock was Christ."—Vs. 4.

"A Living and Dying Prayer for the Holiest Believer in the World" was the first title for one of the most loved of all hymns, "Rock of Ages." Few hymns, if any, have a similar background. It was born out of argumentation, debate and criticism, and first written and published in the *Gospel Magazine* in 1776, edited by Augustus Montague Toplady.

Toplady was very frail. His body held up for only thirty-eight years under the strain of his fiery zeal. He tells that he was converted at the age of sixteen under the ministry of a poor preacher who could scarcely write his name. His conversion took place in Ireland in a service held in a barn, with only a few people present.

An avowed Calvinist, he fell into controversy with John Wesley, the then champion of the Arminians. The battle waged long and hot between these two theologians, even though Wesley had obtained prominence in England and was fifty years Toplady's senior.

The poem that we now know as "Rock of Ages" was a part of this debate. It is interesting to know that Toplady published a book of songs and included in it "Jesus, Lover of My Soul," by—you guessed it—John Wesley.

> **Rock of Ages, cleft for me,**
> **Let me hide myself in Thee;**
> **Let the water and the blood,**
> **From Thy wounded side which flowed,**
> **Be of sin the double cure,**
> **Save from wrath, and make me pure.**

There are three more stanzas.

Though Augustus Toplady and John Wesley were very strongly opposed to each other's theology, each maintained his Christian character and his love for the other.

It is one thing to disagree and quite another to be disagreeable. You and I can disagree "agreeably" with our Christian brothers and remain friends.

Reflection: If your friends disagree with some of your actions, philosophies and standards, listen to them, consider their advice, and then, through the Holy Scriptures, be led of God.

Promise of Help

Hold the Fort

II Corinthians 4

"We are troubled on every side, yet not distressed; we are perplexed, but not in despair; Persecuted, but not forsaken; cast down, but not destroyed."—Vss. 8, 9.

P. P. Bliss was well on his way to fame equal to that enjoyed by Ira Sankey and Fanny Crosby combined. He not only had a golden baritone voice but was also a prolific songwriter. However, a tragic train accident took the life of this young singer on December 19, 1876, when he was only thirty-eight years of age.

Once Mr. Bliss heard Major Whittle tell of a battle waged during the Civil War. On October 4, 1864, just before Sherman began his famous march to the sea, his army lay camped in the neighborhood of Atlanta. General Hood's men very carefully gained control of the rear of Sherman's army and began to cut off supply lines, burn blockhouses and capture small garrisons of soldiers. Then General Hood moved swiftly toward the large post at Altoona Pass.

General Corse of Illinois was stationed there with fifteen hundred men to protect the large store of rations. General Hood sent word for General Corse to surrender, but Corse refused, and a terrible battle ensued.

After many had fallen at their posts and a continuation of the battle seemed futile, a Union officer caught sight of a white signal flag on the top of Kennesaw Mountain, a great distance away. The signal was answered, and very shortly from mountain to mountain this signal was flashed: HOLD THE FORT; I'M COMING. W. T. SHERMAN.

The Union men held on for three more hours until Sherman's forces came up and forced the retreat of Hood's Confederate forces.

Less than twenty-four hours after hearing this story, P. P. Bliss wrote the song "Hold the Fort," the title of which is inscribed on his monument at Rome, Pennsylvania. This is stanza one of four stanzas:

> **Ho, my comrades! see the signal**
> **Waving in the sky!**
> **Reinforcements now appearing,**
> **Victory is nigh.**

Chorus:

> **"Hold the fort, for I am coming,"**
> **Jesus signals still;**
> **Wave the answer back to Heaven,**
> **"By Thy grace we will."**

Reflection: If things look dark today, remember that Jesus knows of your battle and will come to your aid. Count it a blessing that you are in a position to rely only on Him. Stay in the fight and look for His deliverance. Also, look for someone else in need and go to his aid in Jesus' name.

Seeing Through Others' Eyes

Beyond the Sunset

Revelation 22:1–9

"And there shall be no night there; and they need no candle, neither light of the sun; for the Lord God giveth them light: and they shall reign for ever and ever."—Vs. 5.

On April 16, 1961, I had the privilege of visiting with Mr. and Mrs. Virgil P. Brock of Winona Lake, Indiana. Mr. Brock told the story behind his renowned gospel song, "Beyond the Sunset."

We were watching a sunset over Winona Lake one evening. With us were Horace and Grace Pierce Burr. Horace had been blind for many years, but he talked about that sunset with us. We went to dinner still talking about that impressive sunset. The lake seemed to blaze with the glory of God. But above that unusual sunset were threatening storm clouds.

As we talked about that sunset, Horace remarked, even though he was blind, "I never saw a more beautiful sunset, and I've seen them around the world."

I said, "Horace, you always talk about seeing."

He said, "I do. I see through others' eyes, and I think I see more than many others see. I can see *beyond* the sunset."

I said, "Horace, that's a great idea for a gospel song," and I began singing:

Beyond the sunset, oh, blissful morning,
When with our Saviour Heav'n is begun.

Cousin Grace spoke up excitedly, "Oh, Blanche, that's a beautiful thought! Go and play it."

Mrs. Brock laid down her fork and went around to the piano close by and began to play. We stopped eating and listened as she finished the entire musical theme.

She came back to the table and resumed eating. I

94

was too excited to eat. I found an old envelope in my pocket and laid it by my plate. We soon had the first verse.

Remembering those threatening storm clouds gave rise to the second verse.

Then I said, "Horace, we ought to have a verse of this song for you and Grace. She has guided you about for so many years in your blindness, with her hand on yours. How would this do?" We then added a third stanza about being guided by His hand.

A fourth stanza about the glad reunion there completed the song.

"Beyond the Sunset" has become one of the most widely used gospel songs in print today.

Reflection: This life with Christ is wonderful—and Heaven awaits us! As blind Horace Burr needed a hand to guide him, so we too, who were blinded by sin, have been guided by the hand of God to life through His Son. Because of this miracle of the new birth, with Horace, we can see beyond the sunset.

She Wanted to Help

Just As I Am

Matthew 11:27–30

"Come unto me, all ye that labour and are heavy laden, and I will give you rest."—Vs. 28.

Probably the most widely used gospel song in America today is "Just As I Am." It has been called the world's greatest soul-winning hymn. This song has influenced many to give their hearts and lives to Christ. A complete volume could be written telling of the wonderful happenings in connection with the singing of it.

Its author, Charlotte Elliott, most of her life suffered the ills of an invalid body. Many times her weakened condition caused her great lamentation. Such was the case in 1836 when her brother, H. V. Elliott, was raising funds for St. Mary's Hall at Brighton, England, a college for the daughters of poor clergy. She wanted so much to have some little part but was hindered by reason of her affliction. Everyone but her seemed able to help.

She then decided to write a poem to help others in her same condition. She remembered the words of a great preacher, Cesar Malan, who had talked to her fourteen years before and urged her to come to Jesus "just as you are." These words helped her find Christ.

The poem she had written was published without her name and was handed to her one day in a leaflet form by her doctor, the latter not realizing that she was the author. Tears streamed down her face as she read the verses. Copies of the poem were being sold and the money given to St. Mary's Hall. She then realized that she had at last had a big part in the building of the school.

Only eternity will reveal the blessings heaped on other lives by this song. She probably would have shouted for joy could she have heard the following story:

During a song service in a church in Atlanta, John B. Gough was asked by a man in the pew next to him what was to be sung. The questioner was a victim of a nervous disease that had left him blind and twisted in body. The poor man joined the congregation in singing "Just As I Am." As they came to the words, "Just as I am, poor, wretched, blind," the afflicted man lifted his sightless eyes to Heaven and sang with his whole soul.

Mr. Gough later said, "I have heard the finest strains of orchestra, choir and soloist this world can produce, but never have I heard music until I heard that blind man sing, 'O Lamb of God, I come! I come!'"

We quote three of the seven stanzas:

> **Just as I am, without one plea,**
> **But that Thy blood was shed for me,**
> **And that Thou bidd'st me come to Thee,**
> **   O Lamb of God, I come! I come!**
>
> **Just as I am, poor, wretched, blind;**
> **Sight, riches, healing of the mind,**
> **Yea, all I need, in Thee to find,**
> **   O Lamb of God, I come! I come!**
>
> **Just as I am Thou wilt receive,**
> **Wilt welcome, pardon, cleanse, relieve;**
> **Because Thy promise I believe,**
> **   O Lamb of God, I come! I come!**

Reflection: The next time you sing this song, think of your real need before the Lord. Christians need to "come" to Him for daily cleansing.

A Simple, Wonderful Thing

Alas! and Did My Saviour Bleed?

I Corinthians 6:12–20

"For ye are bought with a price: therefore glorify God in your body, and in your spirit, which are God's."—Vs. 20.

"If God has no more service for me to do through grace, I am ready; it is a great mercy to me that I have no manner of fear or dread of death. I could, if God pleases, lay my head back and die without alarm this afternoon or night. My chief supports are from my view of eternal things, and my sins are pardoned through the blood of Jesus Christ."

Those are the words of a man who holds one of the highest positions among hymn writers.

Isaac Watts was born July 17, 1674, at Southampton, England, into the home of "nonconformists," in the days when Dissenters and Independents were persecuted by the Church of England. Fortunately, this intolerance lasted only a short while after his birth. His father, twice jailed during the persecution, afterward prospered in his business and was able to give his son the best in education.

Isaac entered the ministry and preached his first sermon at the age of twenty-four.

His utter lack of what is commonly known as handsomeness was probably why he remained unmarried. Yet I'm sure this frail soul had learned the truth of the verse which begins this meditation.

He wrote many scholarly papers that were used in several institutions of higher learning, but one of the most memorable offerings that came from his pen was a simple hymn "Alas! and Did My Saviour Bleed?"

Fanny Crosby testified that this song helped her find the Saviour when "believing" came most difficult. Countless other individuals have been blessed and helped by this masterful composition.

Alas! and did my Saviour bleed?
  And did my Sovereign die?
Would He devote that sacred head
  For such a worm as I?

Was it for crimes that I have done
  He groaned upon the tree?
Amazing pity! grace unknown!
  And love beyond degree!

But drops of grief can ne'er repay
  The debt of love I owe;
Here, Lord, I give myself away
  'Tis all that I can do.

Reflection: May every step of our existence be guided by the stark realization that we can be in God's will only as we yield to Him that which He rightfully owns—our very lives.

Sing My Song for Me

He Leadeth Me

Psalm 23

"The LORD is my shepherd; I shall not want. He maketh me to lie down in green pastures: he leadeth me beside the still waters."—Vss. 1, 2.

On the northwest corner of Broad and Arch Streets in Philadelphia stands an office building of the United Gas Improvement Company. On the front of this building is a bronze tablet paying tribute to a great hymn and its author, Joseph Gilmore.

In 1862, Mr. Gilmore was guest speaker for a couple of Sundays and one Wednesday evening prayer service at the First Baptist Church of Philadelphia. At the Wednesday service, March 26, he used Psalm 23 as a text, dwelling mostly on the phrase, "He leadeth me beside the still waters." Since the Civil War was in full swing and things looked dark, this subject was especially dear to his heart that night.

After the service, Gilmore and his wife returned to the home of Deacon Wattson, which was next door to the church. That evening the subject of conversation was the same as that of the service—the leadership of God. As they talked, Mr. Gilmore took a pencil and paper and began to write. When he had finished, he handed the verses to his wife and thought no more of them.

Three years later he went to the Second Baptist Church of Rochester, New York to candidate for the pastorate. Upon entering the chapel, he picked up a hymnal to see what type of songs they used. To his amazement, the first song his eyes fell on was his own, written in the home of Deacon Wattson!

His wife, without telling him, had sent the verses to the

Watchman and Reflector, a paper published in Boston. William Bradbury set the verses to music.

Mr. Gilmore had the people of Rochester sing the song so he could hear how it sounded.

In 1926 the First Baptist Church of Philadelphia and Deacon Wattson's home were torn down and an office building constructed on that site. In memory of and appreciation for the song and its author, the gas company placed the bronze tablet on the front. The inscription begins with the first stanza of Mr. Gilmore's great song, "He Leadeth Me."

> **He leadeth me, oh, blessed tho't!**
> **Oh, words with heav'nly comfort fraught!**
> **Whate'er I do, where'er I be,**
> **Still 'tis God's hand that leadeth me.**

Chorus:

> **He leadeth me, He leadeth me!**
> **By His own hand He leadeth me.**
> **His faithful foll'wer I would be,**
> **For by His hand He leadeth me.**

> **Lord, I would clasp Thy hand in mine,**
> **Nor ever murmur nor repine,**
> **Content whatever lot I see,**
> **Since 'tis my God that leadeth me!**

There are two other verses. Get out your hymnal and let them bless your soul.

Pause for a moment with this thought: God wants to lead you in your daily walk. He uses several methods to give His children guidance and leadership: the Bible, pastors, Christian counselors, circumstances and impressions from Him gained through prayer and being open to His will.

Reflection: Wherever He leads you, He has gone before. The Good Shepherd will not lead His sheep in places too hard, so trust Him every step you take.

Something Wonderful From the Kitchen

The Old Rugged Cross

John 19:13–22

"And he bearing his cross went forth into a place called the place of a skull, which is called in the Hebrew Golgotha: Where they crucified him, and two other with him, on either side one, and Jesus in the midst."—Vss. 17,18.

When polls are taken to determine what are the most popular American hymns, invariably near the top of the list is "The Old Rugged Cross." The popularity of this hymn started during the Billy Sunday campaigns in the earlier parts of the twentieth century. Some claim that the song was written between December 29, 1912, and January 12, 1913. What is certain is that it has been by far the most popular of the approximately three hundred songs written by George Bennard, who lived from 1873 to 1958.

Bennard was born into a very modest family in Youngstown, Ohio. His father passed away during George's teen years, leaving the youth with the tremendous responsibility of helping his mother and his brothers and sisters. To that end he became a coal miner like his father before him.

The Salvation Army, which has been a helper of others for so many years, was an attraction to Bennard and his young wife, who joined their ranks and worked with the Army for a number of years.

Bennard later felt impressed of the Lord to become an itinerant evangelist in a time when it was tough to be on the road. He served for years in Canada and some of our northern states. It is also reported that he felt puzzled that others of his hymns did not become as accepted and used by masses of people as "The Old Rugged Cross."

Bennard had a favorite Scripture verse, John 3:16, which he quoted often. He said that it did not become worn or threadbare to him with the oft quoting of it but more alive and deeper in meaning. He seemed always to have a vision of a cross when quoting the verse—a crude Roman cross, stained with the blood of Christ, God's only Son, who gave His life for our salvation.

One day, as he was thinking of that scene, an original melody ran through his mind—"a complete melody," he later reported—but very few words came with it. He struggled to write lyrics, but all that came were the words, "I'll cherish the old rugged cross."

The song seemed to take shape in bits and pieces. He completed the chorus, but the verses did not seem proper and fitting to him. Shortly thereafter he preached in the Friends Church in Sawyer, Wisconsin and the Methodist Church in Pokagan, Michigan, in the southwest part of the state. During those meetings he sang his song for the people, and they responded favorably, but he was not satisfied.

Following the meetings in Pokagan, he was scheduled to speak in New York State, where he majored on the theme of the cross. Numbers of people were trusting in what Christ had done for them on the cross as payment for their sins, confessing Him as their Saviour. Bennard felt that the Lord was revealing to him, in a more meaningful manner, Christ's love as demonstrated at Calvary.

He returned to his home in Albion, Michigan, thrilled with the experiences in New York and with a renewed meaning of the cross etched into his mind and heart. He went to the kitchen table, took the manuscript on which he had so labored, and in just a short period of time was able to rewrite the stanzas, each word falling perfectly into place. He called his wife and joyfully sang it to her. She loved the song very much.

He then sent the manuscript to Charles H. Gabriel in Chicago, asking him if he would write the proper chords with the melody line. Gabriel did so and returned the song with the message, "You will hear from this song." Others who heard the completed song were also very pleased and made similar predictions.

Bennard said what I have heard countless other song-writers say, "I really hadn't written it. I was merely the instrument that God used."

A State of Michigan Historic Site marker stands in the site on Michigan Avenue in Albion where Bennard wrote the song. It reads:

Birthplace of "The Old Rugged Cross"

"The Old Rugged Cross," one of the world's best-loved hymns, was composed here in 1912 by the Rev. George Bennard (1873–1958). The son of an Ohio coal miner, Bennard was a lifelong servant of God, chiefly in the Methodist ministry. He wrote the words and music to over 300 other hymns. None achieved the fame of "The Old Rugged Cross," the moving sum-mation of his faith.

So I'll cherish the old rugged cross,
Till my trophies at last I lay down;
I will cling to the old rugged cross
And exchange it someday for a crown.

George Bennard lived his retirement years in Reed City, Michigan. His last trip to Albion, where he wrote the song, occurred in June 1958 just a few months before his death in October. The first verse of his song:

On a hill far away stood an old rugged cross,
The emblem of suff'ring and shame;

**And I love that old cross where the dearest and best
For a world of lost sinners was slain.**

Reflection: How marvelous that Christ's cross of shame became to you and me a badge of honor and the pain and suffering that He endured there was for our eternal deliverance!

Stand!

Stand Up, Stand Up for Jesus

Ephesians 6:10–18

"Wherefore take unto you the whole armour of God, that ye may be able to withstand in the evil day, and having done all, to stand. Stand therefore, having your loins girt about with truth, and having on the breastplate of righteousness."—Vss. 13, 14.

The year 1858 will long be remembered in Philadelphia as the year when great revival came and when a great gospel song was written.

Dudley A. Tyng was one of the prominent leaders in this great spiritual awakening. Early in that year he was speaking to a crowd of five thousand men, using as his text, "Go now ye that are men, and serve the LORD" (Exod. 10:11).

One report says conviction was so great that at the close of the service two thousand men fell to their knees. Two other writers say that at least one thousand made confession of Christ as Saviour.

A few days after that service, Mr. Tyng was at work in his study. For a few moments of relaxation he decided to walk down to his barn to watch a corn-shelling machine in operation. While he patted a mule being used to operate the machine, the animal became frightened and leaped forward, knocking Tyng into the machine. His sleeve got caught in the cogs. Before they could stop the machine, Tyng's arm was pulled in. It was so badly lacerated that it was amputated.

He lived only briefly after the accident. Just before he died, his dad, leaning over his preacher boy, asked him if he had a message for the young men with whom he had been working. He replied, "Tell them to stand up for Jesus."

George Duffield, Jr., a young pastor and close friend to

Mr. Tyng, was so moved by that message, he preached a sermon the following Sunday exhorting his congregation to stand firm for Jesus Christ. His text was Ephesians 6:14: "Stand therefore, having your loins girt about with truth, and having on the breastplate of righteousness." At the close of the sermon he read a poem he had written:

> Stand up, stand up for Jesus,
>> Ye soldiers of the cross,
> Lift high His royal banner;
>> It must not suffer loss.
> From vict'ry unto vict'ry,
>> His army shall He lead,
> Till ev'ry foe is vanquished
>> And Christ is Lord indeed.
>
> Stand up, stand up for Jesus,
>> The trumpet call obey;
> Forth to the mighty conflict,
>> In this His glorious day.
> Ye that are men now serve Him
>> Against unnumbered foes;
> Let courage rise with danger
>> And strength to strength oppose.

There were six stanzas in all. Benedict D. Steward, the superintendent of the Sunday church school, had some leaflets containing the poem printed for the children. A copy found its way to a Baptist paper, and it was set to music written sometime earlier by George J. Webb.

Almost every hymnal today contains this great song, "Stand Up, Stand Up for Jesus." It has found its way into the hearts of men everywhere, in many lands, causing them to have courage—courage to stand up for Jesus!

Reflection: As in 1858, our day needs men willing to stand up for Jesus—men willing to be leaders. Remember, when you follow the crowd, you will not have a crowd following you.

The Story Wanted; the Story Told

Tell Me the Old, Old Story

Matthew 28:1–20

"Go ye therefore, and teach all nations, baptizing them in the name of the Father, and of the Son, and of the Holy Ghost."—Vs. 19.

When Katherine (Kate) Hankey passed away in 1911, many of her former Sunday school pupils—pupils she had taught fifty years earlier—traveled long distances to attend her funeral. This gives some indication of the tremendous influence that this lady carried.

She was a banker's daughter who, at the age of eighteen, began her work for Christ by starting a Sunday school class for salesgirls. Later she also started one for those of her own social standing. From both classes came many people who yielded themselves to God and His service.

In January of 1866 she became quite ill and spent many months convalescing. During this recovery period she wrote a poem that she later called "The Old, Old Story." At first she wrote only eight stanzas of four lines each and called them "The Story Wanted." Later, in November of that year, she finished the poem, bringing the number of stanzas to fifty, and called the second part "The Story Told." It is said that any number of hymns could be chosen from the many verses.

In 1867, at a convention of the Young Men's Christian Association in Montreal, William H. Doane saw Major General Russell of the English forces stand and read the poem with tears streaming down his bronzed cheeks. Doane was so moved that he wrote a musical setting for the poem and called the song "Tell Me the Old, Old Story."

Here is the first of four stanzas:

Tell me the old, old story

> **Of unseen things above,**
> **Of Jesus and His glory,**
>   **Of Jesus and His love;**
> **Tell me the story simply,**
>   **As to a little child,**
> **For I am weak and weary**
>   **And helpless and defiled.**

Chorus:

> **Tell me the old, old story,**
> **Tell me the old, old story,**
> **Tell me the old, old story**
> **Of Jesus and His love.**

Little did he realize at the time that it would be sung by millions in many lands and be translated into many languages.

Miss Hankey once made a trip to Africa to take care of her invalid brother who had gone there as a missionary. During her stay in this darkened continent, she became so burdened for foreign missions that she gave all of the royalties from her publications to mission work.

Reflection: It is not surprising that one whose life was marked by unselfishness would leave to the world a song like this. It is an "old, old story," but one that is so magnificent and life-giving that each time it is repeated, it seems to be new.

To the Down-and-Outer

The Church's One Foundation

Matthew 16:6–20

"And I say also unto thee, That thou art Peter, and upon this rock I will build my church; and the gates of hell shall not prevail against it."—Vs. 18.

Stainless in character, strong in body, steady in nerve, studious in learning and swift to the defense of the Gospel are said to be characteristics of one Samuel John Stone, born in England in 1839.

His tender heart led him to the down-and-outer, the man on the other side of the tracks. He was a great leader of his people and was loved by them all.

Even in his later years he enjoyed a remarkable ministry among the shop hands and office workers of London. As the early, cheaper trains began to stream into the city bringing the workers, Samuel Stone would open his church and have periods of singing and short messages for the people. He then would allow them to sit quietly and visit, sew or read until it was time for them to begin their day's work.

He noted that many used the Apostles' Creed in their praying, but that few had any comprehension of its meaning. This ignorance, coupled with the blasphemy of the evolutionist and materialist of his day, prompted Stone to write one of the truly great hymns used in our churches today, "The Church's One Foundation."

> **The Church's one foundation**
> **Is Jesus Christ her Lord;**
> **She is His new creation**
> **By water and the Word.**
> **From Heav'n He came and sought her**
> **To be His holy bride;**
> **With His own blood He bought her,**
> **And for her life He died.**

110

No hymn could be more scriptural. In the first stanza the writer tells that the foundation of Christ's church is Himself, that a man must be born of water and the Word and that Christ gave Himself for His church and purchased her with His own blood.

Reflection: It is not enough to know about Christ. In order to go to Heaven, we must know Him and become His. When we give Christ His rightful place, the rest of our theology seems to fall in place.

Tragedy on the Mission Field

God Understands

Isaiah 35

"And the ransomed of the LORD shall return, and come to Zion with songs and everlasting joy upon their heads: they shall obtain joy and gladness, and sorrow and sighing shall flee away."—Vs. 10.

In the mid 1930s tragedy struck a young missionary family when they were all set to leave Peru for a furlough in Canada. Clifford Bicker and his young wife, Ruth, age twenty-six, had been blessed of the Lord with two children during their time in South America.

Shortly before they were to sail for home, Clifford was killed in an automobile accident. The tragic news traveled quickly to the bereaved wife's brother, Dr. Oswald J. Smith, who immediately sent her a poem he had written to comfort her in her hour of heartache. The poem was "God Understands."

When Ruth Smith Bicker and her two fatherless children reached Canada, she told her brother of the comfort the reading of his poem had given her. He then decided to share it with others.

He sent it to B. D. Ackley, asking him to write a musical setting. Mr. Ackley complied, and the result was a great song of comfort, "God Understands."

Dr. Smith, the founder and for nearly thirty years the pastor of Peoples Church of Toronto, Canada, traveled and preached in sixty-six foreign countries.

Yes, Dr. Smith in his lifetime did many wonderful things, but none greater and more lasting than giving to the world songs such as "Then Jesus Came," "The Song of the Soul Set Free" and "God Understands."

Reflection: "The happiest, sweetest, tenderest homes are not those where there has been no sorrow, but those which have been overshadowed with grief and where Christ's comfort was accepted. The very memory of the sorrow is a gentle benediction that broods ever over the household, like the silence that comes after prayer. There is a blessing sent from God in every burden of sorrow."—J. R. Miller.

Traveling With Buffalo Bill

When They Ring the Golden Bells

John 14:1–14

"And if I go and prepare a place for you, I will come again, and receive you unto myself; that where I am, there ye may be also."—Vs. 3.

As we go along from day to day, we meet many who can do at least one thing well. Few and scattered, though, are those versatile individuals who can do many things masterfully.

One such person is the subject of this story. His real name was Daniel A. DeMarbelle, later changed to Dion DeMarbelle. He was born in France on July 4, 1818. He joined himself to a whaling ship and roamed the Arctic Ocean for several of his early years. In 1847 he joined the American Navy and fought in the Mexican War. The following years, though, were probably even more exciting because this is when he really entered upon his versatile career.

Immediately after the Mexican War, he toured the country with an opera company as an actor and singer. When Mr. Bailey, of Barnum and Bailey fame, first organized his circus, DeMarbelle was one of the first performers. He later organized his own show but was forced to close it when fire destroyed his tents in Canada. After this, he turned to helping Colonel William Cody ("Buffalo Bill") establish his Wild West Show.

It has been reported that he could speak on any subject extemporaneously, displaying an unusual amount of eloquence and oratory. To add to this, he was a sleight-of-hand artist, a poet and a composer of popular ballads. And he sang in a Methodist church choir.

Like many men who have achieved fame and fortune, he wasn't satisfied with his contribution to mankind; he wanted to leave something lasting. He did—the words and music to this song: "When They Ring the Golden Bells."

> **There's a land beyond the river**
> **That we call the sweet forever,**
> **And we only reach that shore by faith's decree;**
> **One by one we'll gain the portals,**
> **There to dwell with the immortals,**
> **When they ring the golden bells for you and me.**

Chorus:

> **Don't you hear the bells now ringing?**
> **Don't you hear the angels singing?**
> **'Tis the glory hallelujah Jubilee.**
> **In that far-off, sweet forever**
> **Just beyond the shining river,**
> **When they ring the golden bells for you and me.**

There are three great stanzas that will touch the coldest heart.

DeMarbelle's last years were spent in utter poverty. Only the generosity of his neighbors kept him alive. Because he had served in the Federal Army in the Civil War as a musician, he was buried in Soldiers' Reserve at Bluff City Cemetery near Elgin, Illinois by the Grand Army of the Republic. The marker at his grave reads: Drum Major D. A. DeMarbelle, 6 Mich. Inf.

Thus ended the colorful career of a man remembered primarily as the author of a song that everybody loves, "When They Ring the Golden Bells."

Reflection: It matters not how talented we are or how many people we know and have known. What really matters is that we be ready when Christ comes for His own.

True Greatness

I Must Tell Jesus

Philippians 4:1–9

"Those things, which ye have both learned, and received, and heard, and seen in me, do: and the God of peace shall be with you."—Vs. 9.

When the roll of great preachers is sometimes called, the name of Elisha A. Hoffman is usually omitted. As men count greatness, this omission is justified, but E. A. Hoffman was nonetheless a mighty servant of God. Almost two thousand gospel songs and hymns came from his pen.

When not working in his study, he could often be found working with the poor in the homes across the tracks. One day he visited the home of one of his parishioners in the hills of Lebanon, Pennsylvania. Sorrow and affliction were frequent visitors at this home. Finding the mother in the depths of sorrow and despair, he quoted verses from the Bible that he thought would console her, but he was unable to ease her distress. Then he suggested that she could do nothing better than take all of her sorrow to Jesus. "You must tell Jesus," he told her.

A light broke across her face, and she cried, "Yes! I must tell Jesus." And she did. After a period of prayer, she rose from her knees a new person.

Mr. Hoffman left immediately with those words ringing in his ears, "I must tell Jesus." He went directly home with this inspiration and wrote "I Must Tell Jesus."

The first and third stanzas are quoted here:

> **I must tell Jesus all of my trials;**
> **I cannot bear these burdens alone.**
> **In my distress He kindly will help me;**
> **He ever loves and cares for His own.**

Chorus:
> **I must tell Jesus! I must tell Jesus!**
> **I cannot bear my burdens alone;**
> **I must tell Jesus! I must tell Jesus!**
> **Jesus can help me, Jesus alone.**

> **Tempted and tried, I need a great Saviour,**
> **One who can help my burdens to bear.**
> **I must tell Jesus, I must tell Jesus;**
> **He all my cares and sorrows will share.**

Few gospel songs have been so dear to me. The tune carries the verses so well.

"Down at the Cross" and "Are You Washed in the Blood?" are two other favorites written by Elisha Hoffman that have echoed across America.

Reflection: Sometimes we forget that God wants to help us even more than we want to help ourselves. He wants to be our Friend—not a buddy or a pal, but a true Friend. Remember, He sat where we sit. He was tempted in all points like as we are.

A Truly Great Man

Onward Christian Soldiers

I Timothy 6:7–16

"Fight the good fight of faith, lay hold on eternal life, whereunto thou art also called, and hast professed a good profession before many witnesses."—Vs. 12.

On a holiday known as Whitmonday (seven weeks after Easter) the children of Sabine Baring-Gould's Sunday school were invited to join the celebrations in the neighboring town of Yorkshire, England. Baring-Gould thought that the children should have a song to sing as they marched along carrying their crosses and banners on the way to Yorkshire, but not finding an appropriate one, he sat up most of the night before the holiday writing verses. By morning he had completed a song they could sing.

He taught it to the children the next day, using as a melody the theme from Haydn's Symphony in D. As they marched along, the children sang:

> **Onward, Christian soldiers,**
> **Marching as to war,**
> **With the cross of Jesus**
> **Going on before!**
> **Christ, the royal Master,**
> **Leads against the foe;**
> **Forward into battle**
> **See His banner go.**

He said in an account of his writing, "It was written in a very simple fashion, without thought of publication. Written in great haste, I am afraid that some of the rhymes are faulty. I am certain nothing has surprised me more than its popularity."

This song, like many others, has gone farther than the writer ever hoped or dreamed. Everywhere, in every coun-

118

try of the world, one may hear the strains of this great Christian march.

No longer is Haydn's theme used, but a wonderful composition by Sir Arthur Sullivan, of Gilbert and Sullivan fame.

The song as it is now, with Sullivan's music and Baring-Gould's verses, is a soul-stirring, fighting song, for real "soldiers of the cross."

> **Onward, then, ye people,**
> **Join our happy throng;**
> **Blend with ours your voices**
> **In the triumph song.**
> **Glory, laud and honor**
> **Unto Christ the King—**
> **This through countless ages**
> **Men and angels sing.**

Baring-Gould fell in love with a young lady of his congregation named Grace Taylor, the daughter of a poor mill hand. With the consent of her parents, he sent her away to school to be educated. Upon her return, they were united in marriage in a most impressive ceremony, with Baring-Gould himself pronouncing the vows.

Many of the great songwriters of the past were men of renowned literary ability, including Sabine Baring-Gould. He wrote and published scores of books on many different subjects. Included in these are books on theology, travel, history, myths and the origin of folk tunes. His most popular writing was his sixteen-volume *Lives of the Saints*.

He and his wife became the parents of fifteen children. When she died, eight years before his death, he had engraved on her tombstone, HALF OF MY SOUL.

When on August 10, 1941, President Franklin D. Roosevelt met with Sir Winston Churchill for the signing of the Atlantic Charter, both chose a hymn to be sung at special services. Churchill selected "Onward Christian Soldiers."

Reflection: Sabine-Gould was a man of marvelous Christian character. He saw what needed to be done, set out to do it and was unusually successful. He just kept pushing on for God, and the result was a life of tremendous usefulness.

The Tune Said She Was Safe

Safe in the Arms of Jesus

Psalm 16

"Thou wilt shew me the path of life: in thy presence is fulness of joy; at thy right hand there are pleasures for evermore."—Vs. 11.

In 1868, William Howard Doane made a quick business trip to New York. He hurriedly took care of a business matter and rushed on to Brooklyn to the home of Fanny Crosby. He found her talking to Mr. William Bradbury, one of the great sacred songwriters of the past. Doane told her that he had written a tune he wanted her to hear. He played it for her on a small organ. When he had finished, she excitedly exclaimed that the tune said, "Safe in the arms of Jesus."

She quickly went to another room and, in a matter of minutes, composed the words to what became her favorite hymn. Little did she realize the peace and joy that would be brought to many hearts by this great song.

For many years, "Safe in the Arms of Jesus" has been used at funerals, but Fanny Crosby did not mean for it to be used primarily in that way. You can be sure that it was her prayer that everyone who heard it would soon be able to sing with her:

> Safe in the arms of Jesus,
> Safe on His gentle breast,
> There by His love o'ershaded,
> Sweetly my soul shall rest.
> Hark! 'tis the voice of angels,
> Borne in a song to me,
> Over the fields of Glory,
> Over the jasper sea.

Then stanza three reads:

Jesus, my heart's dear Refuge,
Jesus has died for me;
Firm on the Rock of Ages
Ever my trust shall be.
Here let me wait with patience,
Wait till the night is o'er,
Wait till I see the morning
Break on the golden shore.

Chorus:

Safe in the arms of Jesus,
Safe on His gentle breast,
There by His love o'ershaded,
Sweetly my soul shall rest.

Reflection: Because Fanny Crosby lived close to God, He allowed her, with only a moment's notice, to be a blessing to multiplied thousands who would live even after her death.

Oh, that we would so live that when we come to the end, we can look back and see that on numerous occasions we were able to be a blessing to others because we kept our hearts in tune with God!

Two Tragedies in One Life

When the Saints Go Marching In

I Thessalonians 4:13–18
"Then we which are alive and remain shall be caught up together with them in the clouds, to meet the Lord in the air: and so shall we ever be with the Lord. Wherefore comfort one another with these words."—Vss. 17, 18.

James M. Black, born in Scotland in 1859, became the victim of two tragedies during his lifetime, yet his days on earth were victorious and fruitful.

Between those two terrible events he managed many accomplishments that live on into this present day, not the least of which was the writing of the musical portion of a song which has become one of the most famous Christian songs in the United States. The lyrics were written in 1896 by a little-known poet Katherine Purvis.

At age eight Black was kidnapped, but he was later rescued by an elderly minister who first took the young lad to his home and then, after finding out more about this terrible event, reunited him with his father.

In his early teens, he became active in various kinds of Christian service. As a young adult he came to America and joined the Epworth League in Williamsport, Pennsylvania, an organization that worked primarily with young people. He later became a Methodist preacher.

While still with the Epworth League, Black wrote a gospel song called "When the Roll Is Called Up Yonder." Although he is well known for that composition, his most famous work is the subject of this story. His unique tune helped launch the unusual song, "When the Saints Go Marching In."

It seems that almost every person in the United States can sing at least a portion of the song or hum the tune of the chorus.

123

> I am just a weary pilgrim
>   Trav'ling through this world of sin,
> Getting ready for that meeting
>   When the saints go marching in.

Chorus:

> Oh, when the saints go marching in,
> When the saints go marching in,
> O Lord, I want to be in that number,
> When the saints go marching in.

The ministerial activities of Rev. James M. Black were cut short by his untimely death in an automobile accident in Colorado in 1936, the second tragedy in the life of the man whose work lives on in the tune he gave us more than a century ago.

Reflection: One phrase of the lyric, "O Lord, I want to be in that number," seems to be sung, for the most part, very lightly and flippantly. What does it mean? Well, it means, "Lord, I want to be one of those who will gain entrance into Heaven when Christians are entering their eternal Home."

I'm sure you want to be "in that number"!

Washington Is Burning

The Star-Spangled Banner

Psalm 33

"Blessed is the nation whose God is the LORD; and the people whom he hath chosen for his own inheritance."—Vs. 12.

It is August 13, 1814, and the citizens of Washington, D.C. watch in horror as their city burns. The White House, the Capitol and most of the other government buildings are ablaze. England and the United States are engaged in the War of 1812.

As the British retreated to the ships anchored in Chesapeake Bay, near the mouth of the Potomac River, they took captive one William Beanes, a prominent physician and friend of Francis Scott Key, a lawyer and plantation owner. Key then secured permission from the government to negotiate for the release of Beanes. Although Key was successful, he and Beanes were detained overnight on the British ship *Minden*. Their enemies feared they had learned of the intention to attack Fort McHenry, near Baltimore.

Key and his party watched as darkness fell and obscured Fort McHenry and the fifty-foot American flag that was flying overhead. They watched until the last gleaming of the twilight. A raging battle began. Cannon fire, rockets and flames allowed glimpses of the flag all through the night. As the day dawned, "Old Glory" could be seen still waving. They rejoiced that the Fort had stood.

So thrilled was Key that he grabbed an envelope from his pocket and began to write what his heart was feeling:

> **Oh say, can you see, by the dawn's early light,**
> **What so proudly we hailed at the twilight's**
> **last gleaming,**

Whose broad stripes and bright stars, through the perilous fight,
    O'er the ramparts we watched were so gallantly streaming?
And the rockets' red glare, the bombs bursting in air,
Gave proof through the night that our flag was still there.
Oh say, does that star-spangled banner yet wave
O'er the land of the free and the home of the brave?

He finished the poem the next day in a Baltimore hotel room, adding several more verses. The original copy is in Walters Art Gallery in that city. The poem, sung to an English tune known in the United States as "Adams and Liberty" and written by John Stafford Smith, became so popular in our country that in 1931 Congress made "The Star-Spangled Banner" our national anthem. The flag that flew over Fort McHenry is now on display in the Smithsonian Institute in Washington, D.C.

Francis Scott Key, a devout Christian, believed deeply in liberty and freedom. It is reported that the slaves he inherited from his wealthy father were freed by him in 1817. Before their release, he helped them with family problems, defended them, at no cost, in the courts and started Sunday school classes for them. He did everything in his power to lighten their burdens.

He died January 11, 1843. Two statues of Key stand in our nation: one over his grave, and another in Golden Gate Park, San Francisco, California. A flag, by order of the government, flies continuously over his burial place in Frederick, Maryland.

Many soldiers in Fort McHenry gave their lifeblood on that fateful night that you and I might be free. Today, multiplied thousands of American men and women lie in

Flanders Field and in countless other burial places where crosses mark their graves, row on row. They too gave their lives for our freedom—freedom to live and work and play without the fear of tyranny.

What a wonderful blessing—this freedom we enjoy!

Reflection: Who is the Author of liberty? the Founder of freedom? You and I can never be really free—free from the guilt of our sins—apart from the freedom that Christ alone paid for with His blood on Calvary's cross. Oh, to be free from guilt, to know that our wrongs have been made right, to know that we are free in our nation and in our souls before Almighty God.

We Need a Pilot

Jesus, Saviour, Pilot Me

Mark 4:30–41

"And he arose, and rebuked the wind, and said unto the sea, Peace, be still. And the wind ceased, and there was a great calm."—Vs. 39.

Many of the great songs of the church compare the path of life to a great voyage on the sea.

Edward Hopper was born in New York City in 1816. He was a very humble man, refusing credit for his contributions in the field of hymn writing. He rarely signed his name to his work. And in the cases where he did, he often used a pen name.

After graduation from Union Theological Seminary in 1842, he held pastorates in Greenville, New York and in Sag Harbor, Long Island. From the Sag Harbor church he returned to his hometown and became pastor of the Church of the Sea and Land, which he served until his death in 1888. During this last pastorate, the kindly old gentleman was busy tending the needs of the men who sailed the seven seas. He wrote songs for them to sing in the services and on their journeys.

How happy is the man who can give himself in service to others! It is said of General William Booth, founder of the Salvation Army, that in his latter years failing health kept him from attending one of the annual conventions. Yet he sent a message to be read there. It simply said: "OTHERS!"

That's what serving Christ is all about—knowing Him, then sharing Him with others.

The song that made Hopper so famous, "Jesus, Saviour, Pilot Me," was sung for nine years before he was known as the author. He wrote six stanzas in all. I quote two:

Jesus, Saviour, pilot me

Over life's tempestuous sea.
Unknown waves before me roll,
Hiding rocks and treach'rous shoal.
Chart and compass come from Thee;
Jesus, Saviour, pilot me.

As a mother stills her child,
Thou canst hush the ocean wild;
Boist'rous waves obey Thy will
When Thou say'st to them, "Be still!"
Wondrous Sov'reign of the sea,
Jesus, Saviour, pilot me.

Reflection: You, if you are a Christian, serve the God who controls the seas, with their ebb and flow, their dashing, tossing waves. Surely He can also calm the tempest in your soul when you feel so helpless. He cares and wants to be your Pilot. So turn the wheel over to Him!

"What Does This Tune Say?"

Blessed Assurance

I John 5:1–13

"These things have I written unto you that believe on the name of the Son of God; that ye may know that ye have eternal life, and that ye may believe on the name of the Son of God."—Vs. 13.

Fanny Crosby is one of the most notable names in hymnology. She penned more than eight thousand songs in her lifetime, which spanned nearly a century—she died in her ninety-fifth year—and most of it was spent in blindness. Not even the loss of her eyesight could render defeat to this courageous soul.

She was born Frances Jane Crosby in Putnam County, New York on March 24, 1820. A doctor, with a lack of proper medical knowledge, applied a mustard plaster poultice to her eyes when she was only six weeks old, robbing her of her sight. Yet she grew to be a cheerful, happy soul with a marvelous attitude, accepting her handicap with an unusual amount of courage.

She often said, "I have a jewel—contentment." When she was only eight years of age she wrote:

> Oh, what a happy soul am I,
>   Although I cannot see;
> I am resolved that in this world
>   Contented I will be.
> How many blessings I enjoy
>   That other people don't!
> To weep and sigh because I'm blind,
>   I cannot and I won't.

130

During her fifteenth year she entered the New York Institute for the Blind, where she made such an impressive record that after graduation she was asked to teach at the Institute, and she did so for eleven years. She told S. Trevena Jackson her little "love story," which he recorded in *Fanny Crosby's Story of Ninety-Four Years,* published by Fleming H. Revell in 1915.

Some people seem to forget that blind girls have just as great a faculty for loving, and do love just as much and just as truly, as those who have their sight.

When I was about twenty, a gifted young man by the name of Alexander Van Alstyne came to our Institute. He was also blind and very fond of classic literature and theological lore, but made music a specialty.

After hearing several of my poems, he became deeply interested in my work; and I, after listening to his sweet strains of music, became interested in him. Thus we soon became very much concerned for each other....I placed my right hand on his left and called him "Van."

Then it was that two happy lovers sat in silence while the sunbeams danced around their heads and the golden curtains of day drew in their light. Van took up the harp of love and, drawing his fingers over the golden chords, sang to me the song of a true lover's heart. From that hour, two lives looked on a new universe, for love met love and all the world was changed.

We were no longer blind, for the light of love showed us where the lilies bloomed and where the crystal waters find the moss-mantled spring. On March the fifth in the year 1858 we were united in marriage.

Now I am going to tell you something that only my closest friends know. I became a mother and knew a mother's love. God gave us a tender baby, but the angels came down and took our infant up to God and

His throne. Van went home to his Father's house in the year 1902.

She wrote using her own name as well as many pseudonyms. The story behind one of her songs is the subject at hand.

One day in 1873, Aunt Fanny, as she was affectionately called, was visiting with a friend, Mrs. Joseph Knapp, a musician of sorts and wife of the founder of Metropolitan Life Insurance Company. During their visit Mrs. Knapp played a tune she had recently written, then asked Fanny, "What does this tune say?" Fanny knelt in prayer. As she prayed, the tune was played again. Suddenly she rose from her prayer and said, "It says, 'Blessed assurance, Jesus is mine; oh, what a foretaste of glory divine!'" Aunt Fanny began to dictate verses to Mrs. Knapp who wrote them down, fitting them to the melody just as we hear it sung today. This is the first of three verses:

> **Blessed assurance, Jesus is mine;**
> **Oh, what a foretaste of glory divine!**
> **Heir of salvation, purchase of God,**
> **Born of His Spirit, washed in His blood.**

Chorus:

> **This is my story, this is my song,**
> **Praising my Saviour all the day long;**
> **This is my story, this is my song,**
> **Praising my Saviour all the day long.**

Other songs written by Fanny Crosby include "Praise Him! Praise Him!"; "Draw Me Nearer"; "To God Be the Glory" and "Rescue the Perishing."

She went to be with the Lord only a few short weeks before her ninety-fifth birthday. On her tombstone in Bridgeport, Connecticut are these words from Jesus' remarks concerning the woman in Bethany, "She hath done what she could."

Reflection: No song that we could sing is more meaningful than one that declares our relationship to the Heavenly Father and at the same time is a song of praise to Him.

"Will I Really Be Well?"

Some Golden Daybreak

I Corinthians 15:51–58

"For this corruptible must put on incorruption, and this mortal must put on immortality."—Vs. 53.

Carl Blackmore passed away in December of 1965 in St. Petersburg, Florida. At that time he was connected with the St. Petersburg School of Music. The following is the story behind the hymn "Some Golden Daybreak," just as his wife wrote it to me in a letter.

While preaching over the radio on the subject of the rapture—the glorious hope of the Christians—the Rev. C. A. Blackmore was outlining some of the wonderful things that will happen to Christians. Their deformities and pains will vanish as they leave this old body of clay and instantaneously take on a glorified spiritual body.

A lady who had been bedridden for twenty-three years heard the message. It seemed too good to be true. She wrote to Rev. Blackmore, inquiring, "Will I really be well? Will all pain and sorrow actually be gone?"

Rev. Blackmore replied, "Yes, my friend, some glorious day when Jesus comes, you will leap from that bed with all the vigor of a youth and never again know pain. Little cripples will be made perfect; there will be no more crying, no more heartaches; all will be peace."

His son Carl, who had already become widely known for his musical achievements, was greatly impressed with the reality of the event; and as he pondered the glorious prospects, the words and melody of the chorus took form in his mind. Simultaneously a melody for some verses was inspired, and so he said to his father: "Dad, you should write some verses for this chorus." They agreed to ask the Lord to give the inspiration and guidance.

After much prayer and meditation, early one morning, unable to sleep as he anticipated the thrill of the rapture, Rev. Blackmore got up and wrote the verses as they are today.

As the song has become known, it has grown in popularity until today it is used by all the leading publishers of gospel songs in America and abroad.

"Some Golden Daybreak" has been recorded by one of the nation's outstanding orchestra conductors.

Reflection: The second coming of Christ is the blessed hope of every Christian. Often our daily trials become somewhat bearable when we reflect on the prospect of His imminent coming.

For a complete list of books available from the Sword of the Lord, write to Sword of the Lord Publishers, P. O. Box 1099, Murfreesboro, Tennessee 37133.

(800) 251-4100
(615) 893-6700
FAX (615) 848-6943
www.swordofthelord.com